Ethics for the Practice of Psychology in Canada

Ethics for the
Practice of
Psychology
in Canada

Derek Truscott
Kenneth H. Crook

THE UNIVERSITY OF ALBERTA PRESS

Published by

The University of Alberta Press
Ring House 2
Edmonton, Alberta, Canada T6G 2E1

Copyright © The University of Alberta Press 2004

National Library of Canada Cataloguing in Publication Data
Truscott, Derek, 1959–
    Ethics for the practice of psychology in Canada / Derek Truscott,
Kenneth H. Crook.

Includes bibliographical references and index.
ISBN 0–88864–422–1

    1. Psychologists—Professional ethics—Canada. 2. Psychology—Moral and
ethical aspects—Canada. I. Crook, Kenneth H., 1960– II. Title.

BF76.4.T78 2004   174'.915'0971   C2004-901643-1

Printed and bound in Canada by
Houghton Boston Printers, Saskatoon, Saskatchewan.
First edition, first printing, 2004

The University of Alberta Press is committed to protecting our natural
environment. As part of our efforts, this book is printed on stock produced by
New Leaf Paper: it contains 100% post-consumer recycled fibres and is acid- and
chlorine-free.

The University of Alberta Press gratefully acknowledges the support received for
its publishing program from The Canada Council for the Arts. The University of
Alberta Press also gratefully acknowledges the financial support of the Government
of Canada through the Book Publishing Industry Development Program (BPDIP)
and from the Alberta Foundation for the Arts for our publishing activities.

DEDICATED WITH LOVE TO ALEXANDRA AND SARA

Contents

11 ■ THE ETHICAL PSYCHOLOGIST   131

Acknowledgments

DEREK WOULD LIKE TO THANK THE MANY STUDENTS WHO SHARED their struggles, questions, and answers and who, by doing so, contributed so much to this book. He also thanks Jean Pettifor for sharing her limitless knowledge and for her encouragement. To Jim Evans and Steve Knish he owes a debt of gratitude he can never repay for the countless hours of good talk; this book is a testament to their support. Ken would like to express his thanks to the partners at Alexander, Holburn, Beaudin and Lang, and in particular to Michael P. Ragona, Q.C., Jo Ann Carmichael, Q.C., and Terry Vos, and to their law librarian Susan Daly. And he would be remiss if he did not express his thanks to Drs. W.E. Cooper and J. Vortel without whose very different contributions this book would not have been possible. We greatly appreciate the encouragement and guidance of Linda Cameron and Mary Mahoney-Robson at the University of Alberta Press. Finally, we would like to thank our copyeditor, Eva Radford, the book's designer, Carol Dragich, and artist Frédéric Eibner, whose work graces the cover and the pages of the book.

Preface

THERE ARE MANY BOOKS DEALING WITH PROFESSIONAL ETHICS FOR psychologists. None of the existing books, however, are written from the Canadian perspective and, therefore, do not reflect Canadian code(s) of ethics, laws, and legislation. In addition to filling this gap by providing a text on professional ethics for Canadian psychologists, a secondary purpose is to prompt the beginnings of a more Canadian ethical identity for psychologists by bringing together what we have in common, most notably the Canadian Code of Ethics for Psychologists (Canadian Psychological Association, 2000), into one book.

Each chapter contains an ethical case vignette. Many of these case vignettes are adapted from actual incidents, but simplified and disguised in a variety of ways for the purpose of illustrating a point and protecting the identity of those involved. As such, they do not represent any actual person or situation and any resemblance is purely coincidental. The only exception to this is when legal cases are presented from public documents.

This book is not intended to address the many special ethical and legal issues related to the psychological research environment. While research issues do not represent any new ethical principles beyond those presented here but, rather, entail practical challenges for the application of the foundational ethical principles presented, those challenges are unique and beyond the scope of this book.

This book has several potential audiences. It is primarily intended for students in professional psychology programs who intend to practice in Canada. It will also be useful for professional psychologists seeking to extend their knowledge about responsible practice, psychologists preparing to practice in Canada who are moving from another country, and psychologists in training either in practicum or internship settings. Its comprehensive approach to the subject matter and its inclusion of the code of ethics and professional guidelines as appendixes make it appropriate for use as the main text in courses in professional ethics or professional issues courses. The book contains an extensive reference list and recommended readings for each chapter, so that readers who want to explore the ethics scholarship in greater depth are directed to the proper resources.

Introduction:
Professional Ethics in Psychology

WHILE THE VAST MAJORITY OF PSYCHOLOGISTS ENTER THE profession because they want to help people and, as such, would not intentionally harm their clients, supervisees, or colleagues, such good intentions will likely not resolve the ethical dilemmas that arise during the course of professional life. In fact, the existence of an ethical quandary in professional life may not even be recognized; the right thing to do may not be clear even with knowledge of the rules and law; or, there may be no right answer. And what might constitute a right answer at one time in history may, ten years later, be perceived as an erroneous moral judgment.

The subject of professional ethics is often perceived by the layperson as a series of rules of conduct; it is felt that knowledge of them, in conjunction with an awareness of the general laws in the area, should be enough to prevent the practitioner from going astray. Under this view, a book consisting of the codes of ethics and conduct of our profession, and Canadian law and legal decisions on the practice of psychology, would be exhaustive of the area. While such a book would be a worthwhile contribution, it would be of use only if ethics were a static subject, reducible to decisions of what is right versus what is wrong.

In order to be an ethical psychologist one needs, first, an *awareness* of situations and circumstances in which ethical reasoning is required; secondly, ethical, professional, and legal *knowledge*; and, finally, the *skills* to arrive at an ethically justifiable decision. The format of the book is structured around that triumvirate of requirements.

. The development of professional ethical awareness is a life-long process and a certain amount of experience is necessary. Ethical case studies are included in an effort to provide the reader with some experience, albeit vicariously. The cases used represent realistic, complex, and sometimes confusing situations that psychologists encounter in their practice and, therefore, tend not to have simple answers, nor necessarily be completely resolvable. They are not intended to embody all of the ethical principles and standards discussed in the chapter in which they appear, but rather to raise issues and facilitate awareness.

The major sources of knowledge used in this book are the Canadian Code of Ethics for Psychologists (Canadian Psychological Association, 2000), the codes of conduct of the provincial and territorial regulatory bodies, and Canadian law and legal decisions. All of the ethical questions that psychologists face, however, cannot be answered by one source. New ethical questions and issues arise more quickly and in greater variety than ethics codes or texts can address them. Furthermore, specific answers to questions of ethics usually depend a great deal on the individual circumstances and require a great deal of thought as to how to apply ethical principles. For these reasons, professional psychologists must become familiar with the foundational issues and principles in each of the areas of ethics, professional standards, and legal standards. These constitute the core knowledge that psychologists need to guide them when a professional consensus has already been reached and the guiding principles to reason ethically when faced with situations for which a professional consensus has not been reached. In addition to this core knowledge, comprehensive attention is devoted to the major critical ethical issues that confront psychologists: informed consent, confidentiality, professional boundaries, competence, providing services across cultures, and social justice. In each of the chapters, psychologists' ordinary ethical responsibilities and some of the more troublesome ethical dilemmas are discussed.

Finally, a model for ethical decision making is presented in order to provide the reader with the skills for ethical reasoning. An important aspect of these skills is an awareness and the ability to express how a decision was reached. With this skill the psychologist moves from merely knowing the difference between what is right and what is wrong, to being able to articulate the path of reason used to arrive at the decision.

ETHICS DEFINED

Ethics is the analysis and determination of how people ought to act toward each other when judged against a set of *values*. Values are organizing concepts that motivate us to prefer one behaviour or outcome over another, but do not prescribe specific behaviours. As such, ethics are primarily *aspirational* in nature and focus on the highest ideals of human behaviour and motivations. Professional ethics are the core values held by the members of that profession and their application to resolving ethically problematic issues or defining acceptable or unacceptable professional behaviour.

Ethics differ from *morality*, which is a poorly defined concept in its common use. Philosophers use the concept of morality to refer to an assessment of a person's actions when judged against a system of ethics. Ironically, the common usage of the concept of morality is almost the opposite of how philosophers use it. In common parlance, morality is used to refer to whether or not a person has firm personal standards of right and wrong, often grounded in religious dogma or standards. Morality therefore tends to refer to an individual standard, based upon upbringing, culture, and (usually) religious affiliation. Although some standards such as "do no harm to others" are almost universally shared across individuals referred to as highly moral, how these standards are interpreted and acted upon tends to vary considerably.

Three main features distinguish pure ethical codes: a) they are based on *principles*, b) the principles have *universality* (are relevant for all members of the group under similar circumstances), and c) appropriate actions can be deduced from the principles by *reasoning*. Two relevant facts must be noted at this point. First, codes of ethics for professionals are typically not pure ethics, but rather some combination of ethics, professional conduct, and legal standards. Second, no existing code of ethics perfectly possesses all three of these distinguishing features. Thus, professional psychologists are dealing with an imperfect system for guiding their decisions and conduct. Despite this imperfection, however, psychologists' code of ethics can provide useful guidance for professional behaviour.

Relationship between ethics, professional standards, and the law

While codes of ethics for psychologists contain statements prescribing and proscribing particular conduct, these really do not properly belong in an ethical code. Such statements belong in professional standards and law. *Professional standards* attempt to bridge the gap between ethics and legal standards. All professional standards should be consistent with the Code of Ethics. The most important of these is the *code of conduct* of each province or territory. The code of conduct contains definitions of minimally acceptable behaviour on the part of professionals and is intended to function as enforceable rules of practice. The rules are definitive and prescriptive, and are the standard against which to judge a psychologist's conduct in such settings as disciplinary hearings. From time to time professional psychology groups will develop *guidelines* for practice. These guidelines tend to address specialty areas or areas that present particular challenges to ethical behaviour. They usually bridge the gap between the Code of Ethics and codes of conduct and integrate specialized knowledge in the area of practice. Guidelines are therefore neither definitive nor enforceable.

The *law* deals with minimum acceptable standards of behaviour for members of a society—the "do's and don'ts" of behaviour. Laws relating to professionals deal with regulatory matters, principally around standards for admission into the profession, as well as case law that embodies societal expectations of our professional behaviour. All Canadian jurisdictions (with the exception of the Yukon) have enacted legislation that identifies these codes and standards as delineating what society can reasonably expect of psychologists. This statutory recognition, in turn, tends to be closely followed by case law. Therefore, the development and dissemination of these codes in effect constitutes a legally sanctioned reification of the ethics of our profession.

Because ethical standards are developed by the profession, and given that legal standards represent the values of a larger group (society), there will be times when professional ethics and standards are not consistent with the law. Such situations can be particularly vexatious. Fortunately, with regard to most professional activities, the law assumes that professional codes of ethics are ethically appropriate, and the courts are therefore extremely reluctant to make rulings that contradict a profession's code of ethics. That is, the law generally attempts to follow psychologists' ethics, and this is where they should turn first for professional guidance.

Descriptive vs. proscriptive

Ethics can be *descriptive* of what members of a professional group *actually* do, and they can be *prescriptive* of what those members *ought* to do. Most codes of ethics attempt to strike a balance between description and prescription. Such a balance is not an easy one to strike, however, and the revision of a code of ethics can become quite controversial among members of a profession. If a professional regulatory body attempts to align its codes of ethics too closely with its practitioners' majority opinion, however, they would have to update their code continuously. Such updating would not be because of an evolution toward more ethical behaviour, but because personal and professional perspectives and attitudes change. The uncertainty that would result from such fluctuations would be harmful to a profession and do nothing to enhance the protection of the public. If their code reflects how the most vociferous or influential members of a profession feel about the issues that arise in the conduct of the profession, it may cease to reflect the shared values of the profession and be ignored or rejected.

Ultimately, a professional code of ethics should not contain anything that is ethically peculiar or unique. Professional codes of ethics do not indicate that different ethical principles apply to that profession. Rather, they indicate that the members of that profession have a distinct expertise and face difficult situations that non-members do not, which requires of them a higher-than-normal level of ethical responsibility. A professional code of ethics should be, therefore, the application of general ethical principles to activities characteristic of, or unique to, the profession.

BEHAVING ETHICALLY

Ethics are an essential guide for professional practice. Yet codes of ethics can never cover every situation and circumstance, and they leave a considerable amount of latitude to the judgment of the professional. Perhaps this is as it should be, given that ethical behaviour is based in large part on choices made by psychologists that deeply affect the lives of those who seek their help. Ultimately, no code can substitute for the active process of being ethical. Psychologists must be willing to engage in the struggle of bewilderment, unique contexts, competing demands, and multiple responsibilities. Having chosen to enter a profession, and upon being admitted to it, one becomes the recipient of the privileges, status, and prestige that the profession affords. This responsibility is ethical in nature, and it is in many ways greater than the ethical responsibility incurred by someone who sells a product, because what psychologists sell typically cannot be touched, weighed, or measured. Psychologists can probably get away with many unethical and even illegal practices if they choose to do so; the risk of being caught and prosecuted is quite minimal. But doing so would violate the essence of being a professional. Behaving ethically means approaching professional activities with ethical sensitivity and being prepared to reason ethically in order to act in ethically justifiable ways. The remainder of this book is devoted to assisting you in achieving this.

Ethics for the Practice of Psychology in Canada

A Client in Need

A psychologist has a client who made a commitment to an eight-session contract for therapy, agreeing to the standard rate set by the provincial association. The client was experiencing severe distress due to a faltering marriage and had decided on individual therapy when her husband refused to join her in marital counselling with a different therapist. After four sessions, the client separated from her husband and financial problems ensued. The client cancelled two appointments before the psychologist phoned her to determine why she had cancelled. In the psychologist's opinion, the client was still in severe distress. However, the psychologist could not afford to see clients without being paid for her services.

QUESTIONS FOR CONSIDERATION

1. What individuals and/or groups would you consider in arriving at a solution to this dilemma?
2. What considerations is each individual/group owed? Why?
3. What is your choice of action? Why?
4. What alternative choice(s) of action(s) did you consider? Why did you not choose them?

SOURCE: From *Companion Manual to the Canadian Code of Ethics for Psychologists,* 3rd ed. (Sinclair & Pettifor, 2001).

1 ■ Ethical Principles and Systems

OUR ETHICS DEFINE US. IF A GROUP OF PRACTITIONERS DESIRES TO be acknowledged as a profession and thereby have society grant them the right to regulate their members, their ethics must be based upon a commitment to ensuring that the members of society who receive the practitioners' services are protected from harm. A code of ethics "professionalizes" an occupation by creating an implied social contract with the public that balances professional privilege with a commitment to consumer welfare (Sinclair, Simon, & Pettifor, 1996). In order to be considered a psychologist in Canada, one must accept and abide by the ethical principals and standards contained in the Canadian Code of Ethics for Psychologists (Canadian Psychological Association, 2000).

ETHICAL SYSTEMS

An ethical system ought to provide a framework by which to guide us to ethically acceptable actions. Such a system must be specific enough that we know what to do, and general enough that we know how to be ethical when we encounter new situations. This is why a discussion and analysis of different ethical systems is necessary for the practitioner. Fortunately, it is not necessary to go into detail regarding all of the competing ethical systems and sub-systems; Canadian society follows almost exclusively the teleological and deontological systems in its social and legal practices.

Teleological

Teleological systems of ethics operate from the perspective of outcomes or goals. They can also be thought of as *consequentialistic* in that they are concerned with consequences. By far the most common and accepted teleological ethical system is *utilitarianism* (Mill, 1833/1985).

Its basic premise is that an act is right if, all other things being equal, it produces or is likely to produce the greatest amount of good for the greatest number of people. A utilitarian approach for psychologists would require that they not follow a code of ethics, but rather that they consider the utility of each possible outcome for each situation that they face. A utilitarian approach underlies the cost/benefit and cost/effectiveness considerations so frequently used by health care administrators in their decision making.

A variant of utilitarianism is known as *rule utilitarianism*, which can be stated as, "We should behave in accordance with rules that, all other things being equal, produce or are likely to produce the greatest amount of good for the greatest number of people." Such an approach has the advantage of allowing a profession to codify rules of ethics, and each professional only then has to know which rule to apply to a given situation.

The greatest limitation of both forms of utilitarianism is that they leave unanswered the question of what counts as "good." Some argue that what is good is *hedonistic* or pleasurable; others argue that what is good is what is *ideal* such as honesty, justice, or beneficence; while others argue that it is some mixture of these.

Deontological

The deontological system of ethics maintains that the rightness of an action depends upon whether it is in accordance with, and is performed out of respect for, certain absolute and universal principles. Autonomy, equality, and justice are examples of such principles. Thus, neither the intention to bring about good results nor the actual results of an act are relevant to assessing ethical worth (Kant, 1959). Its basic premise is, "Act as if the maxim of your action were to become a universal law of nature."

Suppose a psychologist motivated by the desire for more money were to prolong services beyond their usefulness. The maxim embodied is such an act would be, "I will provide services whether needed or not in order to make money." Because no one would consent to being so treated themselves, the deontological argument goes, no rational being would accept such a practice as universally binding.

The difficulties with a deontological approach to ethics come from two sources. First, there is no consensus as to which principles are universal and absolute. Second, situations arise whereby principles are at odds with one another. So one might argue that the principle of humanitarianism requires that we lie to persons dying of an incurable disease in order that they maintain their hope in the future, while another would argue that the principle of autonomy requires that we not withhold information that they might use to make decisions about how to conduct the rest of their lives.

Teleological and deontological systems compared

Clearly each system has its strengths and weaknesses. The teleological system provides us with a calculative framework of weighted parameters that allows implementation in an objective fashion. Furthermore, it facilitates the use of social and family-based considerations that allow the placement of the treatment of the client in the social context in which she or he is embedded.

The calculative framework of teleology, however, is also the greatest weakness of the system. By focussing on the social good—greatest amount of good for the greatest number of people—utilitarianism allows for the sacrifice of the individual in the name of the common good. Such an "ends justifying the means" approach stands against the basic value that our society places on the fundamental worth, rights, and duties of the individual. We tend to place a fundamental emphasis on the individual person as a being of ultimate worth, and tend to believe that questions of right or wrong should be decided with reference to universal and absolute principles that preserve, within limits, the autonomy of the person.

FOUNDATIONAL ETHICAL PRINCIPLES

Systems of ethics will only take us so far in our efforts to be ethical practitioners. Whether a teleological or deontological system is employed, psychologists need a set of basic ethical principles that can serve as further guidance for professional behaviour. Five ethical principles have become generally accepted as being centrally important for the helping professions: autonomy, beneficence, nonmaleficence, fidelity, and justice (Beauchamp & Childress, 2001; Kitchener, 1984).

Autonomy

The ethical principle of autonomy deals with respect for the right of the individual to make *choices* about self-determination and to have freedom from the control of others. The word literally means "self rule" and originally referred to the independent self-governance of

Greek city-states (Beauchamp & Childress, 2001). Note that there is an important distinction between freedom of action and freedom of choice: while people should have the freedom to make choices, their freedom of action is limited by the autonomy of others. So one may accept an individual's right to want to harm another person, but one does not accept their right to do so because that would interfere with the autonomy of the intended victim. Respect for autonomy in the practice of psychology is most clearly expressed in our allowing clients to decide for themselves whether or not to undertake psychological services (see Chapter 5).

Nonmaleficence

Nonmaleficence has a long history arising out of medical practice (although it is not contained in the Hippocratic oath as is often thought). It means not causing others harm. In more general terms for professionals, nonmaleficence means not inflicting intentional harm nor engaging in actions that risk harming others, as well as being obligated to protect clients against harm. Most ethicists agree that, all other things being equal, our obligation to protect and not harm our clients is stronger than our obligation to contribute to their welfare (Beauchamp & Childress, 2001). In the medical arena the concept of harm tends to be less controversially understood as physical bodily damage, pain, or death. Psychologists rarely deal in such matters, except in cases of suicidal and homicidal clients, and are more likely to be involved in instances of mental harms or thwarting significant personal interests such as reputation or privacy. There is much less agreement about our obligations with respect to these non-physical harms, especially when we consider such "harms" as annoyance or humiliation.

Beneficence

The principle of beneficence involves actively contributing to the well-being of others. At a basic level that applies to all members of a society, it involves the responsibility to provide aid to those who are in need of assistance. For members of a helping profession, it includes establishing and maintaining a minimum level of competence in order that professional services might be delivered in a manner that furthers the welfare of our clients (see Chapter 8). In some respects nonmaleficence and beneficence can be thought of as being on a continuum from not harming others to benefiting them, with beneficence placing a correspondingly greater demand on us to take positive action, rather than merely refraining from harmful acts (Beauchamp & Childress, 2001). In addition to providing benefit, beneficence also obligates psychologists to balance the potentially beneficial consequences of an action against the potentially harmful ones, particularly the autonomy of their clients. Many a client refuses to accept their psychologist's good advice!

Fidelity

Faithfulness, loyalty, honesty, and trustworthiness fall under the principle of fidelity and are at the core of the fiduciary relationship between helping professionals and the recipients of their services. This principle is particularly important to psychologists because it is the foundation for trust, which is at the core of the bond between people, and because of the power differential inherent in the professional-client relationship. Upholding the ethical principle of fidelity involves placing the interests of our clients ahead of our own, even when doing so is inconvenient or uncomfortable. Fidelity also extends to relationships with colleagues and other professionals. Psychologists have a responsibility to honour contracts with employers, for example, and to act in accordance with the rules of our profession.

Justice

Justice is the ethical obligation to act fairly. In the context of professional ethics it refers to fairness and equity in the allocation of and access to professional services that are scarce, as well as avoiding bias or unfair discrimination in our professional actions. Justice issues are dealt with in detail in chapters 9 and 10.

THE CANADIAN CODE OF ETHICS FOR PSYCHOLOGISTS

History

Immediately after the Second World War, Canadian psychologists found themselves in high demand because of their significant contribution to the war effort and a social-political climate that wanted psychological services (Dunbar, 1998). Just what constituted a "psychologist," however, was open to considerable interpretation, with many persons working as psychologists in various settings having no post-secondary education, or having degrees in disciplines other than psychology (Bois, 1948). In an effort to establish standards of certification, the Canadian Psychological Association (CPA) arranged with the American Psychological Association (APA) to have the American body certify Canadian psychologists who were CPA members. The APA agreed to do so provided, among other things, the CPA adopt a code of ethics (Wright, 1974). The CPA's response was to spend the period from 1949 to 1959 attempting to develop a Canadian code of ethics, which it failed to do, and it eventually adopted the APA's existing code in 1963 (Dunbar, 1998).

By the late 1970s, Canadian psychology had grown to the point where practitioners were expressing dissatisfaction with the APA code because it did not address the concerns unique to Canada. In particular, psychologists in Canada were being employed in community-centred mental health settings as "community psychologists" in roles that were quite different from American psychologists. In 1978 the CPA decided once again to undertake the development of a "made-in-Canada" code.

Development
The Canadian Code of Ethics for Psychologists (Code of Ethics) is particularly unique in that it is based on the "collective wisdom" of Canadian psychologists (Sinclair et al., 1987). Thirty-seven hypothetical ethical dilemmas were constructed to reflect the ethical principals contained within the 1977 APA code of ethics and conflicts between them. The dilemmas were further designed to cover the areas of applied psychology, teaching, and research, as well as traditional and emerging issues and approaches. In order to sample psychologists' ethical reasoning, rather than just their solutions, respondents were asked six questions about each dilemma:

1. Indicate the individuals and/or groups that need to be considered in arriving at a solution to the psychologist's dilemma.
2. Take each of the individuals or groups in turn and explain in detail what considerations each is owed and why. (Think of the rights and responsibilities involved.)
3. What is your choice of action? Why?
4. What alternative choice(s) of action(s) did you consider? Why did you not choose them?
5. What is the minimal circumstance you can conceive in this situation that would lead you to a different choice of action? What would your action be? Why?

6. Do you have any further thoughts or comments about the above or similar situations? Please explain.

Some four hundred Canadian psychologists listed in the CPA membership directory were invited to participate in the study. An effort was made to recruit psychologists with a particular interest in ethics as evidenced by their being on ethics committees or declaring ethics as a special interest in the membership directory, but the majority were selected randomly. One hundred twenty-five indicated a willingness to do so, and dilemmas that corresponded to their stated area of psychology as listed in the CPA membership directory (teaching, research, or applied) were sent to them. Fifty-nine Canadian psychologists returned the questionnaires. The investigators originally asked participants to respond to four dilemmas, but the return rate was so low that they reduced the number to two. An average of five responses per dilemma was obtained.

A content analysis of the responses was then conducted to look for reasons for certain courses of action (e.g., "Psychologists have a responsibility to inform clients of service limitations that might arise due to interference") or values held by the respondent (e.g., "Clients have a right to choose their own therapist"). The statements obtained were then categorized into groups that were ultimately deemed to represent four overarching ethical principles:

Principle I   Respect for the Dignity of Persons
Principle II   Responsible Caring
Principle III Integrity in Relationships
Principle IV Responsibility to Society

Each principle was elaborated upon in a values statement that outlines a number of values subsumed under the principle, derived primarily from the responses to the hypothetical dilemmas. Each principle is further described by a number of standards that demonstrate application of the principle and its values.

Although the principles and values of the Code of Ethics were derived mainly from the participants' responses, additional sources were enlisted for the development of the standards. Psychology ethics codes of other countries, proposed guidelines around ethical issues, and scholarly ethical writings were also reviewed, and additional standards were developed and incorporated under the appropriate principle. This is why standards exist for situations that were not dealt with in any of the hypothetical dilemmas.

The draft Code was then circulated to groups and individuals within and outside the discipline of psychology for feedback. This consultation process resulted in a renaming of one of the principles and a refinement of the values statements and standards, but the principles and their ordering were not altered.

Principle I: Respect for the Dignity of Persons
This principle was given the highest weight of the four principles. It is described in the Values Statement:

> Psychologists accept as fundamental the principle of respect for the dignity of persons; that is, the belief that each person should be treated primarily as a person or an end in him/herself, not as an object or a means to an end. In so doing, psychologists acknowledge that all persons have a right to have their innate worth as human beings appreciated and that this worth is not dependent upon their culture, nationality, ethnicity, colour, race, religion, sex, gender, marital status, sexual orientation, physical or mental abilities, age, socio-economic status, or any other preference or personal characteristic, condition, or status.

Respect for the Dignity of Persons corresponds to the foundational ethical principles of autonomy and, to a lesser extent, justice.

Principle II: Responsible Caring
This principle was given the second highest weight, after Respect for the Dignity of Persons. Responsible caring embodies the foundational ethical principles of beneficence (that psychologists' activities will benefit their clients) and nonmaleficence (at least, do no harm). It also includes standards for balancing risks against benefits, correcting harm and, somewhat incongruously, caring for animals in research.

Principle III: Integrity in Relationships
This principle was assigned the third highest weight and is described in the Values Statement:

> The relationships formed by psychologists in the course of their work embody explicit and implicit mutual expectations of integrity that are vital to the advancement

of scientific knowledge and to the maintenance of public confidence in the discipline of psychology. These expectations include: accuracy and honesty; straightforwardness and openness; the maximization of objectivity and minimization of bias; and, avoidance of conflicts of interest. Psychologists have a responsibility to meet these expectations and to encourage reciprocity.

Integrity in relationship corresponds to the foundational ethical principle of fidelity.

Principle IV: Responsibility to Society

This principle was given the lowest weight of the four principles. It does not correspond directly to any of the five foundational ethical principles. It does address ethical duties associated with beneficence, in that psychologists are expected to increase knowledge and promote the welfare of human beings. Principle IV goes beyond beneficence as normally conceived, however, by broadening the ethical duty to society as a whole, thereby incorporating elements of justice. Principle IV is discussed in greater detail in Chapter 10.

An analysis

Given that no system of ethics is perfect, one would certainly not expect that any professional code of ethics would be perfect either. So how well does the Canadian Code of Ethics for Psychologists embody the ideals presented earlier in this chapter?

The Canadian Code of Ethics for Psychologists, due to the unique method by which it was developed, is predominantly descriptive, as it was intended to be. Although never tested empirically via a survey of Canadian psychologists, one would expect that the profession would readily endorse the principles and standards contained within it. It is difficult, again due to a lack of research, to know the extent to which the Code is prescriptive. It is likely that the psychologists who completed the very time-consuming task of responding to the ethics vignettes, and thereby provided the material from which the code was developed, were highly ethical or at least very interested in ethics. It is therefore likely that the Code contains principles that set a high standard for Canadian psychologists and are more of a prescriptive nature. In addition, some of the content of the Code was derived from existing codes of other countries and ethical scholarship. Such sources also suggest a more prescriptive nature.

While the manner in which the Code was developed can be seen as its greatest advantage, ironically it could also be seen as its greatest disadvantage. The fact that most psychologists agree on a certain course of action or agree to be bound by certain rules of behaviour does not establish that the psychologists are correct or that the rules are ethically valid. They may be, but that could be a matter of pure coincidence. The only study undertaken to date to test the validity of the Code did find that pre-professional psychology students endorse solutions to ethical dilemmas consistent with the ordering of the four principles (Seitz & O'Neill, 1996). In fact, in the absence of reference to any external standards or ethical principles, our Code could well have been ethically unsound. Fortunately, the Code is not purely descriptive but, rather, strikes an appropriate balance between description and prescription.

Minimal behavioural standards do not rightly belong in a code of ethics, as has already been argued. They properly belong in a code of conduct, which is discussed in the next chapter. The Canadian Code of Ethics is organized around four basic principles, which are elaborated upon in corresponding values statements. These value statements articulate the values inherent in each principle, as a code of ethics ought to do. Each principle further contains a great number of standards that are intended to illustrate the application of the values to the activities of psychologists. They range from minimal to more idealized behavioural expectations. While these standards are useful from a practical point of view, they also dilute the pre-eminence of the principles they represent. One suspects that psychologists consulting the Code for guidance, particularly if faced with a pressing ethical dilemma, will tend to refer to standards rather than the values statements. This criticism aside, the Code is based on principles that are relevant for all members of the group under similar circumstances, and appropriate behaviour can be deduced from the principles by reasoning.

The greatest strength of the Code is its basis in deontology. Indeed, its very structure is based upon four principles of ethics. This is consistent with the predominant laws and social norms of Canadian society. Interestingly, the Code even addresses the major criticism of deontology in that it presents a ranked ordering of the principles in order to assist decision making when ethical principles are in conflict. While certainly not a perfect ranking, the Code also includes a decision-making model for further assistance to the professional (see Chapter 4).

SUMMARY

Ethics represent the core values of a profession. Because psychologists claim to be professionals and thereby seek to be granted the right to practice independently, they must abide by a code of ethics that strives to ensure their clients are protected from harm. Professional ethical behaviour, therefore, is predicated on considering the client's welfare as paramount. The major ethical systems are teleological (consequence-based) and deontological (principle-based). The Canadian Code of Ethics for Psychologists was developed by asking Canadian psychologists how they resolve ethical dilemmas. Their responses were organized under four main ethical principles: Respect for the Dignity of Individuals, Responsible Caring, Integrity in Relationships, and Responsibility to Society. Although ethically eclectic, the Code is primarily descriptive, aspirational, and based on a deontological ethical system.

DISCUSSION QUESTIONS

1. What do you think are the relative advantages and disadvantages of a teleological vs. a deontological ethical system as applied to psychological practice? What do you like or dislike about each system?

2. Do you agree with the view that respect for the dignity of persons should be the primary principle governing the ethical practice of psychology? Why or why not?

3. Do you think that the Canadian Code of Ethics for Psychologists should have prescriptive statements? Alternatively, should it be comprised of only descriptive principles? Why?

4. When the Code of Ethics conflicts with the law, the Code indicates that psychologists may follow the law. Do you agree with this position? Why or why not?

RECOMMENDED READING

Beauchamp, T.L. & Childress, J.F. (2001). *Principles of biomedical ethics.* Oxford, England: Oxford University Press.

Canadian Code of Ethics for Psychologists (Appendix A). Preamble: "Introduction," "Structure and derivation of code" and "Uses of the code"; Principle I: "Values statement"; Principle II: "Values statement"; Principle III: "Values statement"; Principle IV: "Values statement."

Dunbar, J. (1998). A critical history of CPA's various codes of ethics for psychologists. *Canadian Psychology, 39,* 177–86.

Sinclair, C. (1998). Nine unique features of the Canadian Code of Ethics for Psychologists. *Canadian Psychology, 39,* 167–76.

Weinberger, A. (1989). Ethics: Code value and application. *Canadian Psychology, 30,* 77–85.

A Psychologist by Any Other Name

You are visiting a private practice psychology agency when you notice a flyer on a bulletin board announcing, "Joan Doe, Ph.D. (Cand.), will be offering a counselling group for men who are divorced." You happen to know Joan and know that she is currently enrolled in the Ph.D. psychology program at your local university. She has a master's degree in career counselling and over twenty years of experience, but has not yet earned her doctorate and is not a registered psychologist. When you ask her what "Cand." means, she says it is an abbreviation of "Candidate," indicating that she is a Ph.D. candidate but has not yet defended her dissertation.

QUESTIONS FOR CONSIDERATION

1. What protection of the public issues are involved in this situation?
2. What ethical values are involved in this situation?
3. Would it make a difference if you were in a jurisdiction where the master's degree was the entry level to the profession? If the Ph.D. was the entry level?
4. If you were to hear this case as a member of your provincial/territorial discipline committee, what consequence would you impose?

2 ■ Professional Standards

THE DEGREE TO WHICH THE PUBLIC CAN TRUST THE PROFESSION OF psychology (or indeed any profession) ultimately rests upon its ability to regulate its members. Every province and territory in Canada, with the exception of the Yukon, has established a professional college to oversee the regulation of the practice of psychology. These colleges are accountable to the public for setting standards for admitting members to the profession and for identifying and sanctioning members who may be at risk to harm or may have harmed a recipient of psychological services. The CPA Code of Ethics encourages psychologists to:

III.36 Familiarize themselves with their discipline's rules and regulations, and abide by them, unless abiding by them would be seriously detrimental to the rights or welfare of others as demonstrated in the Principles of Respect for the Dignity of Persons or Responsible Caring.

III.37 Familiarize themselves with and demonstrate a commitment to maintaining the standards of their discipline.

III.38 Seek consultation from colleagues and/or appropriate groups and committees, and give due regard to their advice in arriving at a responsible decision, if faced with difficult situations.

THE NATURE OF PROFESSIONAL STANDARDS

Entrance standards

One of the more obvious tasks of professional colleges is to set entrance standards deemed necessary to offer psychological services to the public under the protected title of "psychologist." For various reasons both political and historical (and a healthy helping of chance), jurisdictions have established idiosyncratic standards. Some jurisdictions allow persons who have obtained the master's degree to call themselves psychologists, others only those who have obtained the doctorate. A few jurisdictions reserve the title of Psychological Associate for those who have a master's degree. Beyond degree status, there are varying requirements for specific coursework and supervised practice prior and subsequent to earning the degree.

With the signing of the Mutual Recognition Agreement in 2001, psychologists who are registered to practice in one Canadian jurisdiction will have their qualifications recognized in any other jurisdiction, enabling properly qualified psychologists to have access to employment opportunities in all provinces and territories. In order to reach this agreement, the eleven signatory jurisdictions had to agree on the threshold level of training necessary to be called a psychologist. This is certainly a step in right direction given that there is no logical reason that psychological services provided to consumers in one geographical region should require different standards of education, training, and skill than in another.

Codes of conduct

Regulators of psychologists must also ensure that properly qualified psychologists practice competently. While some jurisdictions employ a code of ethics for these regulatory functions, as discussed in Chapter 1, their aspirational nature makes them poorly suited for the task. Regulatory codes of conduct do a much better job of protecting the public welfare by setting a minimum standard of professional behaviour. Effective codes of conduct have several characteristics (from Association of State and Provincial Psychology Boards, 1990):

1. They deal with the psychologist's behaviours within the professional relationship, not the content of professional judgment. They set the parameters within which the

professional relationship functions and are not intended to determine or dictate professional judgment as such.

2. They primarily protect the public interest. They secondarily protect the interests of the profession only as they assure public confidence and trust in the predictability of the professional relationship.

3. They are as non-intrusive as possible; interfering as little as possible with professional work while still accomplishing their necessary function of protecting the public from harm.

4. They are as unambiguous as possible concerning what behaviour is acceptable and what is not.

5. They are sufficient unto themselves, without dependence for interpretation on additional explanatory materials.

6. They are non-optional, non-aspirational, and non-trivial, to the extent that any violation is basis for formal disciplinary action.

As with entry-level competence, each provincial and territorial college has the authority to establish or adopt a code of conduct. All jurisdictions in Canada, with the exception of New Brunswick, the Northwest Territories, and Saskatchewan, have done so. Manitoba, Newfoundland, Nova Scotia, and Prince Edward Island have adopted the CPA's *Practice Guidelines for Providers of Psychological Services* (CPA, 2001; see Appendix B); Ontario developed its own code of conduct which was also adopted by Nova Scotia; British Columbia has developed its own code of conduct; Prince Edward Island has adopted the Association of State and Provincial Psychology Boards' (ASPPB) 1990 *Model Rules of Conduct*; Alberta has adopted a modified version of the ASPPB's 1990 *Model Rules;* and Quebec has developed its own code of conduct. An important practical concern that arises out of this situation is that psychologists who access employment opportunities in more than one province or territory are responsible to practice in accordance with the code of conduct of the jurisdiction in which they are working.

Professional guidelines

Given that the Code of Ethics sets aspirational standards, and codes of conduct set minimal standards, guidelines are used to bridge the gap between the two. Obviously, they should be consistent with both codes of ethics and conduct, while going further to integrate specialized knowledge into standards of quality practice (Sinclair, 1993). Although they are neither usually definitive nor enforceable in and of themselves, regulatory colleges and the courts will often refer to them to establish what the profession sees as desirable practice. Professional guidelines are developed to provide guidance in general areas that are of concern to all psychologists, such as the Canadian Psychology Association's *Guidelines for Non-discriminatory Practice* (CPA, 2001; see Appendix C), and in specialized areas that present specific difficulties, such as the *Guidelines for Psychologists Addressing Recovered Memories* (CPA, 2001). In either case, psychologists should be familiar with guidelines published by their regulatory college, the Canadian Psychological Association, and any speciality organizations relevant to their area of practice.

PROFESSIONAL ACCOUNTABILITY

Various formal mechanisms have been established within the profession and by law to protect the public from harm by psychologists. Ideally, professional standards for accountability should be sufficient to deal with the vast majority of situations. In those rare instances when our standards and mechanisms are not sufficient, external (i.e., legal) mechanisms can be invoked (see Chapter 3). In Canada there are two means by which psychologists deal with professional misconduct: professional ethics committees and provincial/territorial disciplinary committees.

Professional ethics committees

Although membership in professional organizations, such as the CPA, is voluntary, it does provide many benefits to its members, such as reduced rates for malpractice insurance. Continued membership, which is dependent upon adherence to the Canadian Code of Ethics for Psychologists and other CPA standards and guidelines, is therefore something of an incentive for members to behave ethically. The committee on ethics of the CPA can negotiate informal resolutions of complaints with mutual consent of the concerned parties, conduct preliminary investigations of complaints made to CPA about the ethical behaviour of CPA members, and make formal ethics complaints to the board of directors when the preliminary investigation concludes that it is warranted (CPA, 1990). The board of directors has the authority to suspend or expel members (CPA, 1990). The CPA will also encourage anyone who makes a complaint against a member to make a complaint with their regulatory college (CPA, 1986).

In reality, such a sanction is probably not much of a disincentive against behaving unethically, especially since most practicing psychologists are not members of the Canadian Psychological Association. Indeed, the Canadian Psychology Association has only once invoked its authority to expel a member, although several psychologists have chosen voluntarily to discontinue their membership when faced with a complaint. In Canada, provincial and territorial discipline committees typically deal with unethical and incompetent behaviour on the part of psychologists.

Provincial or territorial discipline committees

In most jurisdictions, the college, a member of the public, or a member of the profession can initiate a complaint. Initially, the complaint may be made orally or in writing, although a written complaint must be made if it proceeds beyond preliminary considerations. Normally, the appointed representative of the college will discuss the complaint with the complainant and inform him or her of the standards the psychologist will be held to and the nature of the discipline process. At this point the complainant may do nothing further, make a formal written complaint, or elect for an informal complaint resolution process (provided the jurisdictional legislation allows for it). If the complaint is of a serious nature, the college may proceed with an investigation regardless of the wishes of the complainant.

If the complainant elects to proceed, and provided the complaint is not obviously frivolous or in bad faith, the college representative will typically send a letter to the named psychologist requesting a response and, if needed, a letter to the complainant requesting further documentation. The college may then appoint an investigator who reviews all materials, contacts any relevant parties, collects any necessary further documentation, and prepares a report summarizing the facts or evidence. In some jurisdictions, trained investigators are employed. In others a member of the college board or of the discipline committee may be assigned. The method of investigation varies with respect to the nature of information necessary to elucidate the complaint, and may include interviews, review of clinical files and other correspondence. The college may also seek legal advice or an expert opinion as to whether any relevant codes or standards have been violated.

Once all necessary information has been gathered, the college typically has the option to dismiss the complaint, initiate a mediated or negotiated settlement, or proceed to a discipline hearing. If the complaint is dismissed, the complainant can appeal, usually to the college board or council. If a negotiated settlement is pursued, the psychologist undertakes whatever actions are agreed to be necessary to remedy the wrongdoing. In some cases this may involve a monetary refund if the complainant was overcharged, for example. In other cases it may involve the psychologist undertaking sensitivity training or upgrading. If the psychologist breaches the terms of the settlement, the College typically will forward the matter to the Discipline Committee. If the terms are completed successfully, the case can be closed.

If the case proceeds to a discipline hearing, the committee will hear evidence from the college and the psychologist. At this point in some jurisdictions the client or complainant becomes a witness and the college becomes the complainant. In other jurisdictions the client or complainant maintains "status" and has the right to legal representation, to question witnesses, and so forth. Typically, legal counsel represents both the college and psychologist. If an expert witness was involved, he or she testifies on behalf of the college and can be cross-examined by the psychologist's legal counsel. In most jurisdictions the psychologist is permitted to call his or her own expert to testify.

The penalties available to discipline committees are diverse, from a written reprimand to revocation of the psychologist's registration. Other possibilities include imposing terms, limits, or conditions on the psychologist's practice such as supervision, fines, and restitution to the aggrieved client, personal therapy, or successful completion of courses or exams.

As the discipline committee acts in a quasi-judicial manner, and may impose rather severe penalties, there is a right of further appeal to the lower courts in each of the provinces and territories. The legislation governing this right of appeal varies between jurisdictions, but most allow the courts to uphold, quash, or alter the committee's decision. In hearing an appeal the courts will often defer to the expertise of the college, and by extension the discipline committee, to govern its own affairs and, thus, even where there has been an error in procedure the result may be upheld.

Complaints against psychologists

It is almost impossible to form a precise idea of how many complaints are handled by provincial or territorial regulatory bodies due to the absence of a uniform system of classifying cases. As many as forty cases per year are handled through negotiated or alternate dispute resolution procedures in some jurisdictions, with many more than that handled informally. But the numbers of complaints that go to a formal discipline hearing are very low, from none to two or three per year in any given jurisdiction. In Ontario, most complaints have been in the areas of assessments (particularly custody and access), harmful dual relationships, insensitive treatment of clients, breach of confidentiality, and billing of fees (Evans, 1997).

CASE STUDY OF A COMPLAINT

Although all jurisdictions in Canada have slightly different rules for responding to complaints about their members, the following case study represents a composite of cases and processes that is fairly typical.[1]

Complaint

The Provincial College of Psychologists receives a telephone call from a woman who alleges that a psychologist verbally harassed her and threatened her physically. She states that she was seeing the psychologist in counselling for eight months. She is requested to make the complaint in writing. She does so and it is received by fax a few days later. An investigation is instigated.

Investigation

The psychologist is contacted and reports that the complainant was in counselling for relationship issues and that he had made a diagnosis of "borderline personality disorder." He admitted that he loaned the client $200 to cover a debt "out of compassion." After the client missed her next scheduled appointment, he contacted her by

---

1 We are indebted to Alexandra Kinkaide and Stan Whitsett for providing much of the material in this case study.

telephone and was surprised by her negative reaction to his call. The client did not return for counselling nor did she provide repayment of the loan. After some time the psychologist again contacted the client to ask for repayment. The client became upset and hung up. The psychologist reported that he and the client met in person on one occasion subsequent to the two telephone contacts and that the client became upset and left. The psychologist's case notes document the counselling sessions and his diagnosis, but do not record the lending of any money or any contact to discuss it.

The complainant reported that she felt harassed and could no longer trust the psychologist. She stated that she felt the psychologist used knowledge of her weaknesses against her. She said the psychologist called her repeatedly over money he had "given" her. She reported that during their face-to-face meeting the psychologist became angry and she felt physically threatened.

An expert opinion was sought. The expert opined that a) the psychologist entered into a dual relationship with client when he loaned her money, b) that he should have been aware of the potential for difficulty in light of his diagnosis of borderline personality disorder, c) he should have known that contact regarding money would upset the client, d) the Code of Ethics and the provincial Code of Conduct specifically address difficulties around dual relationships, and e) it is not accepted practice to loan clients money.

Following a review of the materials produced by the investigation, a discipline hearing was scheduled.

Discipline hearing
The discipline committee ruled that a dual relationship existed that violated professional standards. The psychologist was found guilty of professional misconduct and ordered to successfully complete a course of study acceptable to the college regarding dual relationships and professional boundaries.

REGULATING OURSELVES
The essence of being a self-regulating profession is that each member is both regulated and a regulator. Remember that this is because psychologists have special expertise that the average member of society cannot understand. All psychologists, therefore, will find themselves at some time faced with having to respond to unprofessional or

incompetent behaviour on the part of a fellow psychologist. The CPA Code of Ethics encourages psychologists to

IV.13 Uphold the discipline's responsibility to society by bringing incompetent or unethical behaviour, including misuses of psychological knowledge and techniques, to the attention of appropriate authorities, committees, or regulatory bodies, in a manner consistent with the ethical principles of this Code, if informal resolution or correction of the situation is not appropriate or possible.

Most psychologists find this a difficult and anxiety-arousing situation. In fact, this is the most frequent type of ethical consultation with which psychologists are presented. The following steps may be of some help when attempting to deal with these situations in an ethical and responsible manner.

Confirm the issue

Firstly, as best as you are able, try to assess the situation dispassionately. Are you certain that you are competent to determine the appropriateness of your colleague's actions? Are your motives personal, as opposed to protection of the public? Do you have direct knowledge of your colleague's actions? You should be very reluctant to act based upon rumours you have heard from others. Similarly, if you are approached by someone who claims to have first-hand knowledge of the unprofessional behaviour of a colleague, you should be helpful and encourage them to take appropriate action but should be careful about how active a role you take.

Consult

Discuss your concerns with trusted peers, making sure to protect the identity of your colleague and any client(s). Do they agree that action should be taken? Are there any professional guidelines or standards relevant to the issue? Does the situation truly fall below acceptable professional standards?

Client's confidentiality

Except in situations that involve a threat of serious physical harm or suspected child abuse (see Chapter 6), the client's right to confidentiality takes precedence over our professional obligation to correct or offset harm. If a psychologist becomes aware of a colleague's behaviour in the context of a professional relationship (such as in a psychotherapy session), therefore, the client's consent to reveal information disclosed in the relationship must first be obtained. If consent is not granted, no further action should be undertaken unless the situation involves a mandatory reporting duty.

Speak with colleague

When the action appears to be primarily a lack of sensitivity, knowledge, or experience, attempt to reach an agreement with your colleague on the issue and whatever appropriate action is to be taken. Your goal at this point should be to correct the problem, not to punish. Try to be calm, respectful, and constructive; imagine how you would like to be treated if you had made a professional mistake and were being confronted. Try to be open-minded and to understand your colleague's side of the story. A face-to-face meeting in professional surroundings is usually best.

Involve others in an action plan

If your colleague is unwilling to address the issue, or if the action is of a seriously harmful nature, such as the sexual exploitation of a client, you should take your concerns to the provincial or territorial regulatory body best suited to investigating the situation and to stopping or offsetting the harm. You should be willing to make a written, signed complaint and/or testify in a disciplinary hearing if you proceed this far. You should record details of your actions and include time, date, and the basic content of any conversations if you reach this step.

SUMMARY

The degree to which the public can trust the profession of psychology rests upon psychologists' ability to protect them from harm caused by their members. Psychologists are therefore accountable to regulate themselves by setting entrance standards to the profession, developing codes of conduct to set minimum standards of competent practice, publishing professional guidelines to facilitate competent practice, and sanctioning members who are at risk to harm or have harmed a recipient of psychological services. One of the more difficult situations psychologists have to deal with is the possible incompetent behaviour of another psychologist. Psychologists who suspect a colleague has harmed or is at risk to harm a client should first ensure that they have adequate knowledge of the issue, consult with others if unsure, attempt to resolve the issue informally with the colleague, and involve others if necessary or if the issue is a serious one.

DISCUSSION QUESTIONS

1. How do you think the profession should deal with psychologists who violate codes and laws because they have a different personal morality? Why?
2. What are the limits of professional codes of conduct?
3. What is the basis of professional codes of conduct, and from what do they derive their binding power?
4. Do you think the entrance standards for psychologists are high enough? Or are they too high? Explain your answer.

RECOMMENDED READING

Bass, L.J., DeMers, S.T., Ogloff, J.R.P., Peterson, C., Pettifor, J.L., Reaves, R.P., Retfalvi, T., Simon, N.P., Sinclair, C., & Tipton, R.M. (1996). *Professional conduct and discipline in psychology*. Washington, DC: American Psychological Association.

Canadian Code of Ethics for Psychologists (Appendix A). Preamble: "Uses of the code," "Responsibility of the individual psychologist," "Relationship of the code to provincial regulatory bodies"; Principle II: II.40, II.41; Principle III: III.36–III.38; Principle IV: IV.13.

Catano, V.M. (1994). Application of the CPA code of ethics: Towards integrating the science and practice of psychology. *Canadian Psychology, 35*, 224–28.

Dobson, K.S. & Breault, L. (1998). The Canadian Code of Ethics and the regulation of psychology. *Canadian Psychology, 39*, 212–18.

Dobson, K.S. & Dobson, D.J.G. (1993). *Professional psychology in Canada*. Toronto: Hogrefe & Huber.

Haines v. Bellissimo

At the age of forty-one Robert Haines was hospitalized
for treatment of chronic schizophrenia under the care of a
multidisciplinary team that included Dr. Bellissimo, a
psychologist. The team believed that Mr. Haines, upon
discharge, had made minimal improvement. Some time
later his wife discovered a shotgun in their garage and
telephoned Dr. Bellissimo who asked Mr. Haines to come
to the hospital for an assessment. Dr. Bellissimo
assessed the risk of suicide as not being imminent and it
was agreed that he would follow Mr. Haines home and
take custody of the gun. When they arrived at the house,
however, Mr. Haines refused to give up the gun. After
more than three hours Dr. Bellissimo was able to
persuade Mr. Haines to surrender the gun. Dr. Bellissimo
spoke to Mr. Haines on the telephone that night and he
seemed to be "all right." The next day Mr. Haines
purchased another gun and committed suicide. His wife
sued Dr. Bellissimo for malpractice.

QUESTIONS FOR CONSIDERATION

1. Do you think that Dr. Bellissimo should have
   foreseen Mr. Haines's suicide?
2. Do you think that Dr. Bellissimo should have done
   more to prevent Mr. Haines's suicide?
3. Do you think the average psychologist would have
   handled the situation differently? If so, in what way?
4. Do you think an expert in suicide treatment
   would have handled the situation differently? If so,
   what are the implications?

SOURCE: Taken from the case of *Haines v. Bellissimo*, 1977, 18 O.R.
(2nd) 177.

3 ■ Law and Legal Standards

HOW SHOULD PSYCHOLOGISTS MAKE SENSE OF LEGAL DECISIONS? Is it necessary to have the legal expertise of lawyers? It is demanding enough to keep abreast of developments in psychology without having to try to keep up to date with court decisions of professional legal responsibility and liability. Psychologists are not trained in law and are not expected to practice law—only to act in accordance with the law. Instead, a basic understanding of the legal system and, more importantly, of how the profession of psychology is perceived by the Canadian courts can serve as a guide to how the courts would likely judge psychologists if their actions were to be brought before them.

CHARACTERISTICS OF THE LEGAL SYSTEM

Law is made, applied, adjudicated, and enforced in an inter-related way by a myriad of people and institutions. Fundamentally the law provides a set of expectations for behaviour that is acceptable for most people most of the time. In this way people can know in advance what is expected of them so that conflicts can be avoided without needing to resort to the courts. The legal system itself, however, is rather more difficult to characterize. Although not all legal scholars would agree, for our purposes we can describe the system's essential features as *adversarial*, *visible*, and *remedial*.

Adversarial

Our system of law pits one party against the other. It is based on the premise that "legal truth" and justice will emerge when both sides in a dispute have an equal opportunity to present their cases and to challenge the other party's evidence and credibility. This adversarial feature is often disquieting to those who are accustomed to less competitive methods of resolving disputes.

In fact, lawyers do have a duty to try to resolve their clients' disputes by agreement before resorting to court action. If they cannot, then they must do their utmost to act as partisan advocates on behalf of their clients within the law and their legal ethics. It is only when a case does reach the courtroom that the full impact of the adversarial system becomes evident.

Visible

The courts are highly bound by tradition and rules of procedure. The idea is to preserve the dignity and decorum of the institution so that the public can depend upon its order and authority. In order for this to impact the public at large, not just those directly involved in the proceedings, the courts are open to the public. It is said that "justice must be seen to be done." While a court may in certain circumstances ban the publication of information about a case or exclude the public entirely from the courtroom in order to protect the people involved, as in the case of children who are victims of sexual abuse, generally an open court is considered to be essential to its function.

Remedial

The legal system is a dynamic combination of parts functioning together for a purpose: to maintain social order by providing remedies to correct a wrong or settle a conflict. When a criminal case (see below) goes to trial, the judge or jury will decide if the accused is guilty or not and, if found guilty, will decide on a sentence. Sentencing can have a variety of objectives, including denouncing unlawful behaviour, deterring the offender, separating the offender from society, rehabilitating the offender, providing reparations for harm done to the victims, and promoting a sense of responsibility in the offender. When a civil dispute (see below) goes to trial, a judge or jury will reach a decision regarding injuries and who is at fault and will normally render a judgment that is combined with an appropriate remedy to rectify the injury or damage. Such remedies include payment of money to compensate for damages, performance or discontinuance of specific activities, or payment of money to punish the wrongdoer.

AREAS OF LAW

The law can be classified in a number of ways. One distinction is between *substantive* and *procedural* law. Substantive law includes laws that define the rights, duties, and obligations of the citizens of the state, while procedural law deals with the procedures by which substantive law is applied. Another important broad distinction is between the areas of *criminal* and *civil* law. Most of the laws that psychologists will come into contact with are civil laws.

Criminal

Criminal law deals with offences as set out in the Criminal Code of Canada (1985) and related federal statutes. A finding of criminal guilt can result in a fine or loss of liberty in jail or prison. Since criminal acts are considered to be offences against the state, the prosecution of these violations is conducted by the state, referred to as the Crown. The role of the court is to adjudicate between the Crown and the accused. To protect the rights of the accused, given such a powerful discrepancy in status, elaborate and detailed procedural regulations exist to ensure that they are treated fairly. These include the duty of a prosecutor not to obtain a guilty verdict, but to further justice.

In Canada the fundamental legal rights of a person are enshrined in the Charter of Rights and Freedoms (1982) which include the right to life, liberty, and security of the person; to be secure against unreasonable search and seizure; not to be detained or imprisoned arbitrarily; to be informed of the reason for arrest; and the right to retain counsel without delay. In addition to these Charter rights, case law and rules contained in various statutes work to promote due process and procedural fairness in criminal prosecutions. Because the Charter and the Criminal Code establish that a person must be considered innocent until proven guilty, it is up to the Crown to prove beyond a reasonable doubt that the accused did what he or she has been accused of.

In the case of crimes committed by young persons between the ages of twelve and eighteen, the Youth Criminal Justice Act (2002) applies. When dealing with non-violent crimes, youths are treated differently from adults, and a wide variety of alternative measures other than custody are set out in the Act. The Youth Justice Court can order a psychological assessment be done with or without the youth's consent and, if necessary, remand the youth for a period of up to thirty days in order to allow that process to be completed. This new Act has extensive provisions on the duty of confidentiality, including disclosures made by the youth during the course of a Youth Justice Court-ordered psychological assessment.

Civil

Civil law involves the resolution of a dispute in which one person has inflicted a wrong upon another, either intentionally or unintentionally, for which damages may be awarded. This area of law is known as *tort*, derived from the Latin *tortus*, meaning "twisted" or "crooked." By remedying the wrong, tort law can serve a number of purposes. It can compensate the wronged through the awarding of damages, it can set standards and control behaviours, it can educate the public, and it can serve as a means for parties to address their differences in a controlled setting. In civil law the complaining party is referred to as the *plaintiff*, while the party responding to the lawsuit is referred to as the *defendant*. It is the plaintiff's burden to demonstrate a valid basis for the lawsuit when it is filed; otherwise the court will refuse to hear the case.

Torts can be intentional or unintentional. Intentional torts involve deliberate interference with another person through battery, assault, false imprisonment, or infliction of mental suffering. In the case of battery, assault, and false imprisonment, it is not necessary for the plaintiff to prove that any loss or injury occurred in order to recover at least nominal damages, only that the conduct was intentional. In the case of emotional injuries, however, the plaintiff must establish that he or she suffered an injury as a result of the defendant's intentional conduct. Psychologists are most likely to be accused of an unintentional tort: harm resulting from negligence.

NEGLIGENCE

Negligence, as the term is used in the legal profession, refers to conduct that fails to meet the standard required of society. In general, it is accepted that a valid basis for negligence must establish five elements. First, there must be a *duty of care* owed by the defendant to the plaintiff. This duty on the part of psychologists typically arises from the professional relationship, but it may also arise from broader duties owed to members of the more general public. Secondly, there must be a failure to provide *reasonable care*. Third, and perhaps most difficult to understand, there must a degree of *causation* between the conduct and the injury, often referred to as a *proximate cause.* Obviously there must be some damage or *injury* to the plaintiff and, finally, there cannot be any conduct by the injured party that would *preclude recovery.*

Duty of care

The duty of a medical practitioner is often traced to the Hippocratic oath, which likely predates the Hippocratic school of philosophy in Greece. This 2500-year-old code of conduct forms the basis of the International Code of Medical Ethics as amended at Venice in 1983. This code sets out that the practitioner owes a duty to act in his or her clients' best interests, that there is a duty of confidentiality, and that she or he shall maintain the highest standards of the profession.

In most cases the duty of care owed to a client by a psychologist arises by virtue of the professional relationship. It is not necessary that there be a contractual arrangement between the parties. But usually at issue is the standard of care required of the practitioner with the classic formulation being that *Crits v. Sylvester* (1956):

> Every medical practitioner must bring to his task a reasonable degree of skill and knowledge and must exercise a reasonable degree of care. He is bound to exercise that degree of care and skill which could reasonably be expected of a normal, prudent practitioner of the same experience and standing, and if he holds himself out as a specialist, a higher degree of skill is required of him than of one who does not profess to be so qualified by special training and ability.

In stating that a legal duty exists, the courts are saying, in shorthand, that in light of all policy considerations a particular standard of conduct is owed by one person to another. In the absence of such a duty, there is no obligation to act in a non-negligent manner. Such duties may be created by the legislature, by the courts, or by the general understandings of everyday existence. What is important to understand is that to state that a legal duty exists is a conclusion, not a statement of a pre-existing fact.

Reasonable care

The question of what constitutes "reasonable care" is ultimately decided by the courts, not simply by the accepted standard of the profession. As Justice Bouck of the BC Supreme Court observed in a medical malpractice case, "If that is the standard of the profession then it is simply not good enough." The relative inexperience of a psychologist is also not a defence; on holding oneself out as a psychologist, you are deemed to meet the same standard of care whether you have been practicing two months or two decades notwithstanding *Crits'* reference to a practitioner of the "same experience and standing." Thus, while experience or specialization may result in a higher standard of care being required, the reverse is not true.

The standard of care is also dependent upon the risks involved to the client; if one is providing services to a client of a group known to be at high risk of suicide, then there will be a greater duty to protect the client against that risk. The highest standard of care will arise when using an experimental or new procedure, which carries with it higher risk to that client due to the inherent uncertainties of its effects.

The standard, however, is not one of perfection; the law recognizes that mishaps can and will take place without necessarily being negligent. Similarly, while a psychologist must remain reasonably knowledgeable of recent developments in the field, liability will not be imposed simply on the basis that he or she failed to read a professional article on the topic six months earlier. Finally, the circumstances in which the client is being treated will be taken into account by the courts; a psychologist working in an emergency situation will likely have to face a lower standard of care than one working under less time constraints, for example.

Causation

The question of causation is often one of the most difficult issues to be resolved in professional malpractice cases and is often the basis for plaintiffs being unsuccessful. Causation has two aspects: factual causation and proximate causation. The classic description of factual causation is that if not for the defendant's negligence the plaintiff would be uninjured. However, in the real world there are often multiple causes for events, or the causes may be suspected but not known for sure. Because of that, the Supreme Court of Canada has emphasized that causation need not be proven with scientific precision and reiterated that the civil law standard is a balance of probabilities (*Snell v. Farrell*, 1990).

Proximate causation recognizes the general societal policy that a defendant should not be responsible for damages that have practically nothing to do with his or her conduct. In addition to factual causation, therefore, the plaintiff must also establish a sufficient degree of proximity between the cause and the damage. The test here is whether the damage is foreseeable by a reasonable person in the defendant's position. However, there is a concurrent legal principle that the defendant must take the plaintiff as they find them, often expressed as the "thin skull" rule. Thus, a psychologist sued by a plaintiff who suffered injury as a result of being especially vulnerable will still be found liable even though a more robust client may have suffered no injuries.

In instances where there are multiple causes for an injury, the defendant will be responsible only for that portion of the harm attributable to his or her conduct. Similarly, where there are multiple defendants, each person will be adjudged at fault to the extent of his or her own involvement.

Even when a plaintiff client can establish that he or she has sustained foreseeable damages as a result of negligence on the part of a defendant psychologist, the client's own conduct may disentitle him or her from remediation under some circumstances. Plaintiffs may not recover damages in personal injury actions when they were acting illegally at the time, for example, driving recklessly. However, the Supreme Court of Canada (*Hall v. Hebert*, 1993) abolished this defence in personal injury actions. Nonetheless, it may still be possible for a defendant to plead that the plaintiff's conduct is such that it would be an affront to the justice system to allow full or partial recovery. Usually, however, the Court will address this issue by apportioning some degree of causation to the plaintiff's conduct.

LEGAL DUTIES OF PSYCHOLOGISTS

A review of the case law in North America, England, Australia, and South Africa reveals that claims against psychologists are increasing both in number and nature. Because of this it is impossible to provide an exhaustive list of potential grounds of negligence; the law is always evolving. Thus only some particular areas of concern are highlighted here.

Suicide

The most obvious duty psychologists have is the protection of their clients' lives. The difficulties posed by the suicidal client and the courts' perception of psychologists' responsibility in such instances are highlighted in the Ontario decision of *Haines v. Bellissimo* (1977). Another recent case where a failed suicide attempt led to an action for psychological malpractice is the British Columbia Supreme Court case of *Stewart v. Noone* (1992).

Mr. Stewart had been hospitalized on a number of occasions and on one occasion took a drug overdose following the loss of a job. In 1987 he sought emergency care for irregular sleep patterns and manic feelings. The hospital referred him to a community care clinic where he denied being depressed. Two days later he was found unconscious outside his hotel and taken to a nearby hospital. He was discharged in the early hours of the next morning, and he proceeded to his home where he unsuccessfully attempted suicide through an overdose of prescription drugs. He called an ambulance and was taken to another hospital where he was seen by the psychiatric assessment unit and admitted. On the following day he requested that he be discharged, denied any suicidal thoughts or depressive symptoms, and stated that he intended to keep his upcoming appointment at the community care clinic. The psychiatrists believed that the suicide attempt was an impulsive act, and he was discharged. Later that day he drove to a parking garage and jumped from the fourth floor. He survived and sued the hospital and the psychiatrists for discharging him prematurely.

The defence argued that Mr. Stewart's suicide attempt was likely the result of long-term drug and alcohol abuse. Given that at the time the patient requested discharge he was no longer intoxicated, and denied any depressive or suicidal thoughts, they argued that his discharge was appropriate. The court ultimately agreed and found in favour of the defendants, reaffirming the legal standard of reasonable care rather than perfection.

Psychotherapy

Claims may also be made against psychologists for damages sustained as a result of the type of psychotherapy provided. In the Ontario case of *S.T. v. Gaskell* (1997) a client argued that as a result of reliving her past sexual abuse as a child without being first provided the proper support systems she resorted to drinking and threatening a number of individuals with a weapon. Her claim included legal fees incurred in defence of criminal proceedings, damage to her motor vehicle caused by her driving while impaired, and loss of potential employment as a constable because of her criminal conviction and lifetime ban from owning a firearm.

The court declined to find liability on the basis that the therapist was able to point to a stable home environment at the outset of the therapy, that the client freely related her past and that there was no indication during therapy that the client was experiencing undue turmoil. Finally, the court did not accept the client's claim that her criminal behaviour was caused by the therapy.

While the issue of professional boundaries is more fully addressed in Chapter 7, there have been a number of Canadian cases where sexual relationships between a psychologist and patient have been found to be acts of negligence in addition to being unethical and unprofessional. In the case of *N.V. v. Blank* (1988) the psychologist was found to have manipulated his client into having sexual relations with him. The court, following a number of earlier decisions, noted that even if a client consents to such acts it still constitutes a breach of duty in a treatment environment in that it is contrary to the clinical best interests of the client. Other cases have gone further and held that even where the clinical relationship has ended, an enduring influence over the client by the psychologist may preclude true consent to sexual acts being provided by the ex-client.

Assessment

The duty of psychologists extends also to accurate assessment of their clients' condition. An interesting line of legal argument has developed in England and Australia, likely to be followed by Canadian courts, where mental health professionals hired by school boards have been sued for failing to properly assess a need for special education. In one English case (*P.H.P. v. Hillingdon London Borough*, 1998) parents sued the district school board for the failure of an educational psychologist to diagnose their daughter's dyslexic condition when she was a child. The parents were unsuccessful in arguing that if their daughter had been properly diagnosed earlier a special teaching program would have been made available and her subsequent difficulties in employment and life skills would have been prevented. The court ruled that damages could be awarded only if an injury is exacerbated by delayed treatment and, therefore, given that dyslexia is not an injury, no damages were awarded. However, the court did note that if the psychologist had been hired privately by the parents, rather than employed by the school board, liability might be found for failure to fulfil a contract.

Underlying this decision is a strong legal view that claims such as these, brought against psychologists many years later, would be counter to the societal interest in providing free education. While there are no reported cases in Canada where this issue has been addressed, under Canadian law there may be instances where liability would be found against a privately employed psychologist. The courts would likely look for a long-term and direct relationship between the client being assessed and the psychologist where it could be shown that the psychologist clearly did not meet the standards of the profession.

Third parties

There can be few, if any, psychologists who are unaware of the *Tarasoff v. Regents of the University of California* (1976) decision and the impact it has had worldwide. In that case, Mr. Poddar, under the care of a psychologist and psychiatrist, confided that he intended to murder Tatiana Tarasoff. The psychologist notified the campus police who decided that there was insufficient basis for having a committal order made. A few weeks later Mr. Poddar murdered Ms. Tarasoff, and her parents sued the psychologist and the psychiatrist. The court ruled that there was a valid basis for the claim to proceed, stating:

> Where a therapist determines, or pursuant to the standards of his profession should determine, that his patient presents a serious danger of violence to another, he incurs an obligation to use reasonable care to protect the intended victim against such danger. The discharge of this duty may require the therapist to take one or more of various steps, depending upon the nature of the case. Thus, it may call for him to warn the intended victim or others likely to apprise the victim of danger, to notify the police or to take whatever steps are necessary under the circumstances.

In Canada, the *Tarasoff* principle has only been addressed directly in the single case of *Wenden v. Trikha* (1991) in which Mr. Trikha was placed under close supervision in a psychiatric ward under the care of a psychiatrist. Shortly after his admission he eloped from the hospital and was involved in a car accident in which Ms. Wenden was seriously injured. Ms. Wenden commenced a civil action against the hospital and the psychiatrist.

The court held that when a psychiatrist becomes aware that a patient presents a serious danger to the well being of a third party or parties there arises a duty to take reasonable steps to protect such a person or persons if the requisite proximity of causation exists. In *Wenden* there was no identifiable victim, making the question of proximity difficult. Ultimately, the court held that the psychiatrist had not acted negligently and thereby the issue of proximity was not addressed.

The Supreme Court of Canada in the decision of *Smith v. Jones* (1999) accepted this approach, and the general principle of *Tarasoff* but noted:

> Two observations should be made. First, it will not always be necessary to identify a specific individual as the victim. Rather it may be sufficient to engage the duty to warn if a class of victims, such as little girls under five living in a specific area, is clearly identified. Second, although Moore J. speaks of the patient "verbaliz[ing] his intentions," I believe it is more appropriate to speak of a person making known his or her intentions. While speech is perhaps the most common means of making intentions known, it is certainly not the only manner of indicating a clear intention. It could be accomplished soundlessly yet with brutal clarity by thrusting a knife through a photograph of the intended victim.

It should be noted, however, that the court was principally concerned in that case on the issue of privilege, and thus this comment is likely an incidental opinion and therefore not binding, although almost certainly to be followed in any subsequent Canadian decision.

An interesting variant of the *Tarasoff–Wenden* duty occurs when it is the therapeutic process itself that causes harm to a third person. The most common instance where this arises is where the client is undergoing psychotherapy for past sexual abuse and the alleged perpetrator brings a civil action against the health care practitioner. In the British Columbia case of *Carnahan v. Coates* (1990) a father sued a psychologist after the psychologist testified in court in favour of the mother's application denying the father's access to their children. The mother had been receiving psychotherapeutic services from the psychologist and persuaded him to interview her children. On that basis the psychologist subsequently gave evidence that resulted in the father's access to the children being substantially reduced.

Counsel for the psychologist successfully applied to have the claim dismissed on the basis that the lawsuit had no valid basis. A number of arguments for striking the claim were rejected by the presiding judge, most importantly the claim that the psychologist did not owe a duty of care to the plaintiff father. The court observed that "the state of law regarding the nature and extent of a professional person's duty towards those who come within the range of foreseeable harm arising from professional misconduct is unsettled" and thereby a suit might proceed on the grounds that the father was owed a duty of care. On the basis that a witness must be free to testify in court without fear of reprisal by civil suit, however, the court held that the psychologist, provided he had no malicious intent towards the father, was immune from suit.

These legal reasons preventing liability from being found when a child is at risk of harm do not arise in cases of recovered memories of sexual abuse, however. This controversial area of practice, where a client in psychotherapy "recovers" previously repressed memories of abuse, largely came into prominence following the publication, and subsequent appearance on the television show "Oprah," by the authors of the book entitled *The Courage to Heal* (Bass & Davis, 1988).

The psychologists who assist clients in recovering their memories of past sexual abuse run some risk of being sued by the alleged perpetrator, even though the psychologists' intent was only to provide therapy to their clients. The leading case in Canada is the British Columbia decision of *I.G. v. Rusch* (1999) where a number of family members who had been accused of sexual abuse sued the accuser's therapist for breaching the duty of care owed to them as persons wrongfully accused. In an application to have the lawsuit dismissed, the court observed that being falsely accused of child abuse is a devastating tragedy and thus there may be good reasons for extending a duty of care from a therapist to a falsely accused third party. However, there are also compelling reasons against such an extension, of the duty, including discouraging the detection, reporting, and treatment of bona fide cases.

The court ultimately concluded that the detection and reporting of abuse are more important societal goals and that it would only be in exceptional circumstances where the court should extend to the duty of care to third parties. In this case, the court refused to make that extension, noting that the therapist had at no time suggested to his client that she confront the family members over the abuse, nor did he either himself report the matters to the police nor encourage the client to do so. The case leaves open the issue as to what the result would have been had the psychologist contacted the police directly, or through his client.

SUMMARY

A basic understanding of the legal system and of the expectations of the profession of psychology by the Canadian courts can serve as a guide to how the courts would likely judge psychologists if their actions were to be brought before them. The Canadian legal system is adversarial, visible, and remedial in nature and deals with disputes either through the criminal or civil courts. If psychologists are involved with the legal system, they tend to be defendants in civil suits, which deal with professional negligence. Negligence involves five elements: a duty of care, a failure to provide reasonable care, an injury, causation between the failure and the injury, and an absence of factors on the part of the injured party that would preclude recovery. Specific legal duties of psychologists exist with respect to suicide, psychotherapy, assessment, and third parties.

DISCUSSION QUESTIONS

1. What is the difference between ethical, professional, and legal standards for professionals?
2. Is a psychologist ever justified in breaking the law? If so, under what circumstances? What system of ethics does your answer represent?
3. What are the limits of legal decisions as a guide for professional behaviour?
4. Given the fundamental differences in how the legal system and psychologists arrive at the "truth," does psychology rightfully have a place in courtroom proceedings?

RECOMMENDED READING

Canadian Code of Ethics for Psychologists (Appendix A). Principle I: I.39, I.42, I.43, 1.45; Principle IV: IV.17, IV.18, IV.27, IV.29.

Gall, G.L. (1995). *The Canadian legal system.* Toronto: Carswell.

Truscott, D. & Crook, K.H. (1993). Tarasoff in the Canadian context: Wenden and the duty to protect. *Canadian Journal of Psychiatry, 38,* 84–89.

Yates, R. A., Yates, R. W., & Baines, P. (2000). *Introduction to law in Canada.* Scarborough: Prentice-Hall Canada.

Child Abuse

You are providing family therapy to Mrs. and Mr. Jones and their two children, aged eleven and thirteen. The family sought therapy because they "argue too much" and have made good progress so far. In the third session the oldest child reports that their father has hit them in anger on numerous occasions over the past ten years. Approximately one year ago the oldest child's arm was broken when Mr. Jones threw him against a wall.

Mr. Jones expresses considerable remorse and asks for your help to reduce his violent behaviour. He says that he was removed from his family when he was a boy because his father was physically abusive and that he could not bear to have his children taken away from him. You are concerned that he will seriously harm himself if the children are apprehended. Mrs. Jones and the children state that they want to remain together as a family and work things out.

QUESTIONS FOR CONSIDERATION

1. What individuals and/or groups should you consider in arriving at a solution to this dilemma?
2. What ethical values are in conflict in this situation?
3. Does this dilemma arouse any strong feelings for you? How might these feelings affect your choice of action?

SOURCE: Adapted from the *Companion Manual to the Canadian Code of Ethics for Psychologists*, 3rd ed. (Sinclair & Pettifor, 2001).

4 ■ Ethical Decision Making

REASONABLE PSYCHOLOGISTS WITH GOOD PERSONAL AND professional values will fairly often find themselves in situations that are difficult to resolve ethically. An ethical dilemma is a situation where it is difficult to know how to behave because there are either conflicting ethical standards that apply, or the nature of the situation (e.g., complex, unclear) make the application of ethical standards difficult.

Most readers will recognize that the situation presented in the case study represents an ethical dilemma. Vulnerable children are in need of protection from further harm. At a societal level it has been acknowledged that the need to protect children from abuse should come before any other need; this is codified as a legal obligation to report a child in need of protection to the appropriate authorities. Not to do so would be to risk legal sanctions that in most jurisdictions in Canada include fines and imprisonment. The psychologist is also in a position to help both the children and their abusive father, however, and the opportunity would most likely be lost if a report was made against their wishes. The purpose of this chapter is to present a model for arriving at a justifiable ethical decision in this situation, and when faced with ethical dilemmas in general.

THE ETHICAL DECISION-MAKING PROCESS

The process of ethical decision making can often be very rapid, leading to an easy solution to the question of how to best behave ethically in a given situation. This is particularly true when one can apply clear-cut guidelines or standards, and when there is no conflict between ethical principles. Ethical dilemmas, however, are not easily resolved, are often emotionally distressful, and typically require time-consuming deliberation. For such dilemmas people need guidance and justification for their decisions.

It can be helpful to be aware of two levels of ethical thinking. The first is the immediate or *intuitive* level of judgment. Such judgments tend to be spontaneous and emotional without any clear, conscious decision making. This intuitive level of judgment, for example, is the basis of the typical psychologist's feeling of outrage when a colleague harms a client. This personal ethical sense is based upon a lifetime of learning about being moral, of which training and experience in professional ethics and standards of practice may constitute only a very small part (as in the case of students). In ideal circumstances, intuitive ethical judgment predisposes psychologists to act in ethically appropriate ways and leads to sound ethical choices. In ambiguous or confusing situations, or when they have strong personal biases, however, their intuitive judgment may not lead to desirable choices or serve as justification for their professional actions.

In order to honour their end of the societal contract that allows psychologists to be self-regulating, their profession requires them to be able to justify their ethical decisions according to principles that serve to protect the public (see chapters 1 and 2). Reliable, justifiable, ethical decisions require that psychologists be able to employ a *critical-evaluative* level of judgment (Kitchener, 1984). A critical-evaluative judgment involves a deliberate process of intensive problem solving based on professional ethical values, principles, and standards that is grounded in a commitment to the protection of the public.

This interrelationship of these two levels of ethical judgment is diagrammed in Figure 4.1. The diagram is arranged to highlight the two different levels of ethical judgment and the importance of the influence of professional standards and consequences. At the immediate, intuitive level, psychologists' ethical judgments are based on their experience of the situation and their personal ethical sense. This level of judgment will normally lead to an ethical choice of action. This choice, however, must be justifiable on professional ethical grounds applied in a systematic manner. Particularly when confronted with new situations, psychologists should proceed through a structured decision-making process such as the one in the CPA Code of Ethics and described in detail in the next section of this chapter. As more and more new situations are encountered and this process is repeated, their personal ethical sense becomes more and

FIGURE 4.1 A MODEL OF ETHICAL THINKING.

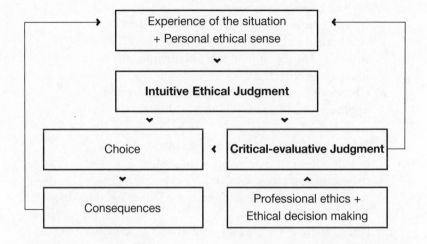

more in alignment with their professional code of ethics through repeated exposure to the values, principles, and standards of the profession and through experience with the consequences of their choices. Thus ethical decisions that are justifiable and professionally appropriate become more intuitive with experience if psychologists practice applying critical-evaluative ethical thinking.

A good way to make justifiable and appropriate decisions is to employ an established model. The CPA Code of Ethics contains just such a model.

A MODEL FOR ETHICAL DECISION MAKING

The Canadian Code of Ethics for Psychologists presents a decision-making model in the preamble to the Code proper. While the Code of Ethics can be used without referring to this model, it is more thorough and comprehensive than any other published models (Cottone & Claus, 2000) and thus represents an excellent choice. The CPA model is comprised of ten steps:

1. Identification of individuals and groups involved or likely to be affected by the decision
2. Identification of relevant ethical principles, standards, and guidelines

3. Consideration of how personal bias, stress, or self-interest might influence the development of or choice between courses of action
4. Development of alternative courses of action
5. Analysis of likely risks and benefits of each course of action for the individuals and groups involved or likely to be affected
6. Choice of course of action after conscientious application of steps 1 through 5
7. Action
8. Evaluation of the results of the course of action
9. Assumption of responsibility for consequences of action, including correction of negative consequences, if any, or re-engaging in the decision-making process if the ethical issue is not resolved
10. Appropriate action, as warranted and feasible, to prevent future occurrences of the dilemma

1. Identification of individuals and groups likely to be affected by the decision

In the simplest case the only parties legitimately concerned with the outcome of an ethical dilemma would be the psychologist and the client. In practice, however, other parties are almost always involved. In some cases a third party, such as an insurance company, is paying for the service. In other cases a psychologist is employed by an agency or institution to provide services. In still other cases a third party, such as a parent or the courts, directs that psychological services be offered. In all situations it is important for the psychologist to be clear about who has a legitimate right to be considered when professional decisions are being made, and to consider what their preferences and interests are.

To return to the example from the beginning of the chapter, the individuals and groups involved or likely to be affected by the psychologist's decision are the children, father, mother, family as a unit, the psychologist, and society in general (via its interest in protecting children and in its valuing psychotherapy).

2. Identification of relevant ethical principles, standards, and guidelines

The next question one should ask oneself is, "Does a relevant standard of conduct, ethical principle or standard, or professional guideline exist?" This question obligates a review of relevant professional documents, starting with the code of conduct for the appropriate jurisdiction, the Code of Ethics (see Appendix A), professional guidelines, and through to the scholarly ethics literature. Indeed, as one student suggested to us, one test of the ethical prudence of a psychologist might be to measure the distance between their office chair and their copy of the CPA Code of Ethics!

In some situations, especially for students and beginning practitioners, one's decision-making efforts may stop at this point when a relevant standard or guideline is found. Even more experienced practitioners may find that a review of their jurisdiction's code of conduct or the CPA Code of Ethics turns up standards that they had missed before or forgotten. The codes are, after all, quite detailed and one may have difficulty recalling specifics when they are hypothetical, and it is hard to imagine exactly how they might apply to situations one had not yet encountered.

If there is no single ethical or professional standard that applies, psychologists must identify the ethical principles or values that are in conflict or that are difficult to apply. Once they have done so, they are sometimes able to identify an overriding or primary ethical principle. With the CPA Code of Ethics the four ethical principles are ordered in terms of their relative importance, making prioritizing conflicting principles somewhat easier. Thus, Principle I: Respect for the Dignity of Persons, should generally be given the highest weight, except in circumstances when doing so would threaten the life of another person. Principle II: Responsible Caring should be given the second highest weight. Principle III: Integrity in Relationships generally should be given the third highest weight. And lastly, Principle IV: Responsibility to Society should generally be given the lowest weight of the four principles when it conflicts with any of them.

In our example, the CPA Code of Ethics encourages psychologists to

I.45   Share confidential information only with informed
        consent, except as required by law, or in circumstances
        of actual or possible physical harm or death.
and

II.39   Do everything reasonably possible to stop or offset the consequences of actions by others when these actions are likely to cause serious physical harm or death. This may include reporting to appropriate authorities (e.g., the police) or an intended victim, and would be done even when a confidential relationship is involved.

Thus one can see that there is a conflict between wanting to ensure that the children are safe from harm (Principle II) and wanting to respect the family's expressed wish that no one else know about the father's abuse of the children (Principle I). Additional considerations are: not wanting to precipitate circumstances that could prompt the father to harm himself (Principle II), honouring a commitment to help the family (Principle III), and respecting society's value of protecting children from harm as well as maintaining the confidentiality of psychotherapy (Principle IV).

3.   Consideration of personal bias, stress, or self-interest

Doing the right thing professionally demands altruistic motives and a commitment to be of service to others. One might even go so far as to say that an ethical psychologist is first and foremost a person of virtue. This does not mean that all psychologists must be saints, but they should regularly consider how their own interests and "blind spots" are influencing their ethical choices. In response to financial stresses, for example, they may make ethical compromises in hopes that no harm will result and they will profit. Sometimes a situation will arouse feelings in them that block their ability to understand and sort through the problem, such as a psychologist who has recently gone through a difficult custody battle of his or her own and finds it difficult to provide a balanced opinion in a custody assessment for a client.

Sometimes psychologists may be able to resolve the personal issue that is interfering with their conscientious application of their professional obligations before attempting to make the ethical decision. In other situations it may be possible to recognize that their personal biases or stresses are an issue, and acknowledge them as something to remain aware of as they proceed through the decision-making process. Seeking consultation from a trusted colleague would be well advised in either case.

When psychologists become aware of self-interests influencing their decisions they should, quite simply, refrain from acting on them. This is not to say that their rights and preferences should be disregarded—they are certainly legitimate parties to the outcome of the ethical decision—but rather to highlight that they should never benefit at the expense of their clients.

In our example, the psychologist may have strong feelings about the importance of family integrity, self-determination and responsibility with respect to suicide, and the protection of vulnerable children. Additionally, he or she may be very concerned about the potential legal risk to the extent that a relatively higher value might be placed on avoiding liability than on helping the family.

4. Development of alternative courses of action

In situations when no single ethical principle outweighs the others, a number of ethical actions may be ethically appropriate. A review of relevant codes and ethical literature, and consultation with colleagues, may be of benefit. Time can be spent "brainstorming" and generating possible solutions that address the conflicting principles without being too concerned with the feasibility of the alternatives at this point. When at all possible, the client and involved parties should be involved in the development of possible solutions.

In our example, there are only two alternate courses of action:

1. Report to the appropriate authorities.
2. Do not report and continue to provide therapy to the family.

5. Analysis of likely short-term, ongoing, and long-term risks and benefits of alternatives

When evaluating the alternative courses of action generated in step 4, one needs to consider to what extent each alternative:

Satisfies the preferences of the affected parties. Given that the Code of Ethics obligates psychologists to promote human welfare by respecting the dignity of individuals first and foremost, in particular cases this translates into promoting the preferences of the involved or affected parties. Thus, if no standard exists that resolves the dilemma, a course of action that satisfies, or at least takes into account, the preferences of affected parties should be developed. This is consistent with the principle of autonomy whereby all other things being equal, psychologists should provide the services that they agreed to provide.

Presents no new ethical problems. The nature of ethical dilemmas is such that attempts to resolve them can present new problems. In particular, one may feel tempted to do something "a little unethical" such as telling a partial truth in order to avoid larger ethical issues. Such alternatives are really based on expediency rather than ethical responsibility. Hass and Malouf (1995) suggest that one consider the "clean, well-lit room" standard: how would you feel presenting your choice of action to a group of your colleagues in a professional setting? If you imagine yourself feeling uncomfortable, perhaps that alternative is not a good one.

Addresses the ethical principles that are in conflict. This consideration may seem obvious, but practitioners often focus on more clinical and practical issues, such as what would be "good for" the client, rather than on the ethical principles that are in conflict, such as autonomy versus beneficence.

Advances one principle over the other(s) in conflict. Again, the nature of a dilemma is that each alternative advances one ethical principle while compromising another. The idea of considering risks and benefits is not to promote a consequentialist approach to ethics. Rather, the best (or sometimes least undesirable) alternative is the one that compromises fewer principles or compromises the conflicting principle(s) to a lesser degree than the other alternatives.

Can practically be implemented. Practicality refers to whether or not one could actually put the alternative into effect. Often, for example, psychologists would like to change social policies or the way they commonly conduct themselves professionally, but cannot implement such changes in a particular case (see Chapter 10). Also, they need to consider how practical a particular alternative is for themselves personally. The time and effort that a course of action may require can sometimes be out of proportion to the ethical dilemma it is intended to resolve.

To return again to our example, if the children's possible need for protection is reported to the authorities the psychologist would not be satisfying the preferences of any of the affected parties except society in general. Indeed, there is a high likelihood that the father will harm himself and that the family will terminate therapy, thereby presenting a new ethical problem. The psychologist would, however, be advancing the ethical principle of offsetting or preventing harm by responding to the children's need to be physically safe from their father's violence.

If the psychologist does not report, he or she would be satisfying the preferences of the family, and they will likely continue in therapy where the psychologist may well be able to help the father reduce his violent behaviour. A new ethical problem may be created, however, if the psychologist is not able to reduce the father's violence, and the children may suffer further harm. Also, the rest of the family may be afraid to tell the psychologist the extent of the father's violence and they may be in more danger than he or she realizes.

6. Choice of course of action

After conscientious application of steps 1 through 5, the psychologist ultimately needs to make a choice. Ideally, the choice will be justifiable to others and his or her own conscience. It may help to remember that no one can be held to a standard of perfection; one must simply try one's best to do the right thing. In our example both courses of action address the ethical principles in conflict, have the potential to create new ethical dilemmas, and can be practically implemented, but have advantages and disadvantages with respect to advancing the interests of the affected parties and advancing one principle over another. Given that the psychologist is dealing with the physical safety of children who are not in a position to champion their own interests, the best course of action is to inform the authorities of their need for protection.

7. Action

Making a decision is not enough; one must act in order to be able to say one is truly ethical. Remember that even not doing anything is a choice. Sometimes taking action can be a relief from the tension of anticipation. Behaving ethically can result in increased work, pressure and anxiety, however. It can also sometimes necessitate defying or confronting others who have power over us, for example, supervisors or employers. Implementing our choice of course of action therefore often involves additional skills, such as assertiveness, fortitude, and the ability to convey respect for all who are affected by our actions.

This is not to say that all choices are unpleasant. Coming to an informed, ethical decision can provide a sense of professional pride and mastery, and instil confidence in our ability to master future dilemmas. It can also provoke respect in colleagues and facilitate a more ethical workplace environment. All reasonable steps should be taken to inform and involve the persons affected by one's actions, and to document the ethical decision-making process.

In our example the psychologist would inform the family of his or her decision and the reasons for it, give them every opportunity to participate, contact the authorities, and do his or her best to maintain a therapeutic, or at least professional, relationship with the family.

8. Evaluation of the results of the course of action

Evaluation of the results of one's actions goes hand in hand with implementation. Ideally, the psychologist will be able to follow-up with all parties affected by his or her actions, although this is not always possible. Certainly the most ethical course of action will not always please everyone, and some people will not want to have further contact with their psychologist. But whenever possible the psychologist should include the direct recipient(s) of his or her services in the ongoing process of evaluating whether his or her actions are ethically appropriate.

In our case example the psychologist would follow-up with the family and the authorities.

9. Assumption of responsibility for consequences of action taken

Although psychologists are expected to consult with others and be guided by professional codes and standards, the responsibility for their actions remains with the individual psychologist. Often, their actions bring to light additional dimensions of the situation, which may lead to a redefinition of the problem, necessitating consideration of further alternatives, and so on.

Hopefully, the family in our example will maintain their trust in the psychologist's intentions to act in the best interests of everyone involved, and the psychologist can continue to provide therapy. If so, he or she would be particularly mindful of the father's suicide risk and intervene as appropriate. If the family does not stay in therapy the psychologist should offer referrals and seek the family's consent to coordinate the transfer of services.

10. Appropriate action to prevent future occurrences of the dilemma

Every experience changes the people involved. Ethical dilemmas tend to change us rather profoundly. Often the emotional toll prompts a psychologist to conclude, "I'm never going to provide that type of service (or to that category of client, etc.) again!" Such a reaction, although understandable, is counterproductive. In fact, what tends to happen when psychologists adopt such an attitude is that they become more rigid in their interactions with clients and have less access to their personal-professional resources. Taking time to reflect on what one has learned from the situation is probably the best means for preventing future dilemmas:

- Are there things that I would do differently next time?
- Am I as familiar as I would like to be with ethical codes, standards, and literature?
- Do I have a professional network with whom I can effectively consult?
- Are there changes that I could or should make in my professional practices that may prevent future occurrences of similar dilemmas?
- Are there changes that could or should be made in the policies and procedures of the institution that may prevent future occurrences of similar dilemmas?

In our example, the psychologist would probably want to consult with colleagues in order to review his or her decision making and to debrief emotionally, and may want to review the profession's informed consent procedures.

SUMMARY

Ethical decisions should be made after careful deliberation. A ten-step model for making ethical decisions begins with (step 1) identification of the individuals and groups potentially affected by the decision and moves to (step 2) identification of relevant ethical principles, standards, and guidelines. In step 3 psychologists consider the influence of any personal biases, stresses, or self-interest, and then (step 4) develop alternative courses of action. Step 5 involves analysis of likely pros and cons of each course of action. At step 6 psychologists choose a course of action, then (step 7) act, (step 8) evaluate the results of the course of action, and (step 9) assume responsibility for the consequences of action. Finally, in step 10, the psychologist takes appropriate action, as warranted and feasible, to prevent future occurrences of the dilemma. Although the process appears time consuming at first, it can be shortened by familiarity with the ethics code, professional guidelines, and the ethics literature; maintaining ready access to knowledgeable colleagues with whom to consult; and experience.

DISCUSSION QUESTIONS

1. Why might psychologists not always behave as ethically as they ought to?
2. How would you decide which colleague(s) to consult with about an ethical dilemma?
3. Under what circumstances would you feel tempted to disregard ethical standards in favour of your intuitive judgment? Under what circumstances would you feel justified?
4. Do you agree with how the ethical dilemma was resolved in this chapter? Why or why not? If not, how would you resolve it?

RECOMMENDED READING

Canadian Code of Ethics for Psychologists (Appendix A). Preamble: "When principles conflict"; "The ethical decision-making process."

Pettifor, J.L. (1989). Did Hamlet need a Canadian code of ethics for psychologists? *Canadian Psychology, 30*, 708–11.

Pettifor, J.L. (1998). The Canadian Code of Ethics for Psychologists: A moral context for ethical decision-making in emerging areas of practice. *Canadian Psychology, 39*, 231–38.

Sinclair, C. & Pettifor, J.L. (2001). Use of the code in ethical decision making. In C. Sinclair & J.L. Pettifor (Eds.). *Companion manual to the Canadian Code of Ethics for Psychologists,* 3rd ed. (pp. 105–43). Ottawa: Canadian Psychological Association.

FREE AND INFORMED CONSENT
CASE STUDY

Parental Refusal

You have undertaken a psychological assessment of a child referred by his parents to address difficulties in school as identified by the child's teacher. The parents have given consent to have their child assessed and to release the test results to the school, which is your normal practice. Upon completion of the assessment you discuss the results and your conclusions with the parents prior to presenting the results to the school. It is your recommendation that their child be given additional tutoring in class, which the school will provide under their policy for children with special needs. The parents then tell you that they do not want the assessment report shared with the school because they do not want their child to be seen as "retarded." Despite your best efforts at explanation and persuasion, they will not relent.

QUESTIONS FOR CONSIDERATION

1. Who is the client in this situation?
2. Who is responsible for deciding what course of action to take in this situation?
3. Are there ethical values in conflict in this situation? If so, what are they?
4. What difference would it make if you were in private practice? If you were employed by the school board?

SOURCE: From *Companion Manual to the Canadian Code of Ethics for Psychologists,* 3rd ed. (Sinclair & Pettifor, 2001).

5 ■ Free and Informed Consent

ALL OTHER THINGS BEING EQUAL, THE RIGHT TO MAKE DECISIONS about whether or not to receive psychological services, and the nature of those services, belongs to the client. This conclusion finds support not only in psychologists' ethical values, particularly the social contract between a profession and society (see Chapter 1), but also in our professional standards (see Chapter 2) and law (see Chapter 3). Informed consent is the most represented value in the Canadian Code of Ethics for Psychologists and includes the following standards:

I.16   Seek as full and active participation as possible from others in decisions that affect them, respecting and integrating as much as possible their opinions and wishes.

I.17   Recognize that informed consent is the result of a process of reaching an agreement to work collaboratively, rather than of simply having a consent form signed.

I.18   Respect the expressed wishes of persons to involve others (e.g., family members, community members) in their decision making regarding informed consent. This would include respect for written and clearly expressed unwritten advance directives.

I.19   Obtain informed consent from all independent and partially dependent persons for any psychological services provided to them except in circumstances of urgent need (e.g., disaster or other crisis). In urgent circumstances, psychologists would proceed with the assent of such persons, but fully informed consent would be obtained as soon as possible.

In principle, therefore, the issue presents no problems. Practice, however, is different than theory: what precisely does the right to free and informed consent involve in practical terms for recipients of psychological services?

CONSIDERATIONS OF PRACTICE

Informed consent means that the client understands the benefits and risks of the service a psychologist may provide and willingly agrees to them. Two parameters are crucial, therefore: how much information should be disclosed and is consent freely given?

Standards of disclosure

It is absolutely essential that the client have the necessary and sufficient information about the service to be provided or recommended. Clients cannot act as autonomous persons if they are unaware of the alternatives from which they must choose or the implications of the various alternatives. Because the average person has no other way to gain this information, psychologists have an obligation to provide it. The need for information is heightened by the fact that most people's presuppositions about psychology often are mistaken. Many people, for example, may believe that psychologists can "read their minds" or dispense medications. Psychologists must, therefore, do whatever is reasonably possible under the circumstances to provide clients or potential clients with adequate and sufficient information so as to allow them to exercise their right. But how much information is adequate and sufficient? There are three possible standards of disclosure to consider: full, professional, and objective.

The standard of full disclosure would require that *all* information relevant to a given situation be provided. Given the impossibility of anyone knowing all the relevant information, such a standard is neither practical nor enforced professionally or legally.

The professional standard requires that the psychologist disclose as much information as a similar colleague would disclose under similar circumstances (*Kelly v. Hazlett*, 1976). The problem with such a standard is it ignores the status of the client as an autonomous agent and places the decision in the hands of the profession. Not surprisingly, the courts revised this standard quite soon after and replaced it with the *objective reasonable person* standard (*Reibl v. Hughes*, 1980).

The objective reasonable person standard holds that professionals have an obligation to disclose whatever a reasonable person would want to know under their particular circumstances in order to make the decision under consideration. This means that psychologists should pay due regard to the *particular* circumstances of their clients from the perspective of the clients' personal, cultural, and other needs and characteristics. It is quite reasonable that a person from a particular background would want to know (or not know) what a person with a different background would not (or would). In a multicultural society such as Canada this is a very important consideration (see Chapter 9). This legal standard is completely consistent with the profession's ethical standards:

I.23   Provide, in obtaining informed consent, as much information as reasonable or prudent persons would want to know before making a decision or consenting to the activity. The psychologist would relay this information in language that the persons understand (including providing translation into another language, if necessary) and would take whatever reasonable steps are needed to ensure that the information was, in fact, understood.

I.24   Ensure, in the process of obtaining informed consent, that at least the following points are understood: purpose and nature of the activity; mutual responsibilities; confidentiality protections and limitations; likely benefits and risks; alternatives; the likely consequences of non-action; the option to refuse or withdraw at any time, without prejudice; over what period of time the consent applies; and, how to rescind consent if desired.

I.25   Provide new information in a timely manner, whenever such information becomes available and is significant enough that it reasonably could be seen as relevant to the original or ongoing informed consent.

I.26   Clarify the nature of multiple relationships to all concerned parties before obtaining consent, if providing services to or conducting research at the request or for the use of third parties. This would include, but not be limited to: the purpose of the service or research; the reasonably anticipated use that will be made of information collected; and, the limits on confidentiality. Third parties may include schools, courts, government agencies, insurance companies, police, and special funding bodies.

III.14 Be clear and straightforward about all information needed to establish informed consent or any other valid written or unwritten agreement (for example: fees; concerns; mutual responsibilities; ethical responsibilities of psychologists; purpose and nature of the relationship; alternatives; likely experiences; possible conflicts; possible outcomes; and, expectations for processing, using, and sharing any information generated).

From an ethical (and legal) point of view, however, it is not sufficient to simply impart information; it must be understood if it is to be used to make a decision. This requires a collaborative stance vis-à-vis the client.

Freedom of consent

Obviously, consent that is not given voluntarily does not represent true consent at all. If the value underlying consent is respect for the dignity of the individual and the right to autonomy, then clients must freely give their consent. Threats of harm or incentives—whether physical, emotional, monetary, or social standing—negate consent. Similarly, manipulation by presenting information in a biased fashion, withholding information, or outright deception, does not represent ethically (or legally) valid consent. The Code of Ethics advises psychologists to:

I.27 Take all reasonable steps to ensure that consent is not given under conditions of coercion, undue pressure, or undue reward.

I.29 Take all reasonable steps to confirm or re-establish freedom of consent, if consent for service is given under conditions of duress or conditions of extreme need.

I.30 Respect the right of persons to discontinue participation or service at any time, and be responsive to non-verbal indications of a desire to discontinue if a person has difficulty with verbally communicating such a desire (e.g., young children, verbally disabled persons) or, due to culture, is unlikely to communicate such a desire orally.

I.36 Be particularly cautious in establishing the freedom of consent of any person who is in a dependent relationship to the psychologist (e.g., student, employee). This may include, but is not limited to, offering that person an alternative activity to fulfil their educational or employment goals, or offering a range of research studies or experience opportunities from which the person can select, none of which is so onerous as to be coercive.

III.32 Not offer rewards sufficient to motivate an individual or group to participate in an activity that has possible or known risks to themselves or others.

Obtaining consent

It may be most helpful to think of informed consent as a process of working collaboratively with a client. That is, the principle of informed consent is never completely satisfied; one must be constantly attentive to whether the professional relationship is a collaborative one. As circumstances change, which is often the very goal of psychological services, so too does the information needed by the client to decide whether or not to continue with the activity.

It is sometimes mistakenly thought that informed consent is dealt with in the first contact with the client and then can be forgotten. Indeed, if a client expresses surprise or dissatisfaction with some aspect of service, psychologists with this mind-set might be tempted to remind them that they had given consent previously! Such a stance does not reflect true, informed consent. Likewise, signed consent forms do very little good from the point of view of the client. They may serve the interests of the psychologist or some other third party by providing documentation that something took place, but even the issue of what the client actually understood they were agreeing to or whether the client felt pressured to consent remains open to argument. Even the Code of Ethics is ambivalent on this issue:

I.21 Establish and use signed consent forms that specify the dimensions of informed consent or that acknowledge that such dimensions have been

explained and are understood, if such forms are
required by law or if such forms are desired by the
psychologist, the person(s) giving consent, or the
organization for whom the psychologist works.

I.22   Accept and document oral consent, in situations
in which signed consent forms are not acceptable
culturally or in which there are other good reasons
for not using them.

Certainly reading a form does not ensure that the content is
understood. Studies of patients who sign consent forms find that
their comprehension and memory of the purpose and nature of the
treatment is poor (Cassileth, Zupkis, Sutton-Smith, & March, 1980:
Robinson & Merav, 1976). Ultimately, the responsibility for ensuring
that consent is truly informed and freely given—whether through
the use of a signed consent form or documented oral consent—is the
responsibility of the psychologist.

From a practical point of view, therefore, psychologists should
explain the purpose and nature of the service to be undertaken, the
reasonably foreseeable benefits and risks, and any alternative courses
of action. This initial discussion should be documented either in
case notes or using a consent form. Once services are initiated,
psychologists should remain alert to indicators of client collaboration
and agreement and discuss them openly with their clients, particularly if reluctance or disagreement is sensed, and document these
discussions.

MINOR AND DEPENDENT CLIENTS

Particularly difficult practical problems arise regarding consent when
providing psychological services to children and dependent adults.
The Code of Ethics advises psychologists to

I.33   Seek to use methods that maximize the understanding
and ability to consent of persons of diminished
capacity to give informed consent, and that reduce
the need for a substitute decision maker.

I.34   Carry out informed consent processes with those
persons who are legally responsible or appointed
to give informed consent on behalf of persons not
competent to consent on their own behalf, seeking

to ensure respect for any previously expressed preferences of persons not competent to consent.

1.35 Seek willing and adequately informed participation from any person of diminished capacity to give informed consent, and proceed without this assent only if the service or research activity is considered to be of direct benefit to that person.

Minor children

Every jurisdiction in Canada has set a legal age of majority. In most jurisdictions that age is eighteen, although in some it is nineteen (Rozovsky & Rozovsky, 1990). Above this age, adult competence is assumed. Below the age of majority, competence to consent is questioned and parental or guardian approval is needed for many activities. Parents have a legal duty to provide care and support for their minor children and the corresponding legal right to direct and supervise them. If the parents know their minor child is receiving services and give consent, the psychologist's task is fairly straightforward. Once parental consent is obtained, the psychologist should provide the minor child with as much information as he or she is able to understand and obtain the child's agreement to proceed.

If a minor seeks a psychologist's services but does not want to obtain parental permission, however, the matter becomes complicated. Common law does recognize the principle of a *mature minor*. Minors can be considered "mature," and thereby provide their own consent, if they have sufficient understanding and intelligence to enable them to fully appreciate the service being proposed (*J.S.C. and C.H.C. v. Wren*, 1986). Although chronological age is only one of several factors to be considered (see *Assessing competence* below), court precedent suggests a benchmark—a minor would likely not be considered a mature minor before the age of fifteen. The competence of minors aged fifteen years and older of average intelligence to understand what they are agreeing to has been established through a variety of research studies (Adelman, Lusk, Alvarez, & Acosta, 1985; Kaser-Boyd, Adelman, & Taylor, 1985; Lewis, 1981; Weithorn & Campbell, 1982). Indeed, on some characteristics they cannot be distinguished from young adults of the age of majority. With children between the ages of eleven and fourteen, caution should be exercised regarding their abilities to understand the complexities and consequences of psychological services, confidentiality, and so on (Weithorn & Cambell, 1982).

If the minor's capacity and understanding of the service is sufficient to warrant being treated as a mature minor, his or her consent is sufficient. This determination must also be balanced against the degree of risk inherent in the situation, however. Situations involving greater or longer-term risks, such as life-threatening sexually transmitted diseases, may ethically justify a greater involvement of parents or guardians than might be the case where risk is trivial. Also, care must be taken with children under the age of fifteen with respect to freedom of consent given their tendency to acquiesce to authority (Grisso & Vierling, 1978; Mann, Harmoni, & Power, 1989).

Other statutory exceptions may apply to the normal requirement for parental consent. Psychologists who work in schools should be aware of the legislation in their jurisdiction. In Alberta, for example, a student under the age of eighteen may be considered "independent" as defined in the School Act and would be considered competent to give consent to psychological services.

An immature minor who does not want to participate in psychological services that his or her parents have consented to on his or her behalf should be provided as much choice as possible around aspects of the service that are negotiable. The psychologist should attempt to build a trusting relationship with the child and thereby secure his or her agreement, provided the service is in keeping with the best interests of the child. Ultimately, if the minor steadfastly refuses to agree to participate in the psychological service, particularly intervention, it will be of little if any benefit and the parents should be so informed. No psychologist should continue to provide a service that does not help the child.

Dependent adults

Persons of the age of majority are assumed to be competent to make decisions for themselves unless proven otherwise. As a society we regularly respect individuals' rights to make decisions that are of questionable benefit to their well-being, such as smoking and consuming unhealthy foods. Equally important is that we normally allow members of our society to make these decisions regardless of any personal characteristics, conditions, or status. At the individual level, therefore, empowering others to decide for themselves should normally be given precedence over promoting their well-being. When a service is for the benefit of the individual, free and informed consent, including the choice of refusing the service, should normally be respected regardless of our opinion of what would promote their well-being. As we have already stated, the only ethically justifiable circumstance in which psychologists would decide for others whether they should be subjected to any form of psychological service is when they are not competent to decide for themselves. The relative weighting of respect for the dignity of the individual (Principle I) over responsible caring (Principle II) is now adjusted by virtue of the individual being unable to make decisions in his or her own best interest. Considerations of self-determination are now subsumed under considerations of well-being. When individuals are incompetent to make a decision for themselves, therefore, the proxy decision-maker should attempt to replicate as much as possible the decision that the client would make under the circumstances if they were competent. The dependent adult's opinions and wishes should also be respected and integrated into any decision as much as possible. In most cases the dependent adult will have a legally appointed guardian. In cases where the individual does not, the psychologist should either petition the court to appoint a guardian to make decisions on the individual's behalf, or seek a family member's consent. The latter is permissible in some jurisdictions, but is less preferable because judicial involvement affords the individual substantially greater protection.

Assessing competence

Competence (or incompetence) does not describe a trait or even state of an individual; it describes an individual's ability (or inability) to perform a particular task. Thus it is decision-relative, not global. A person may be competent to make a particular decision under certain circumstances, but not competent to make a different decision, or even the same decision, under different circumstances. Assessing competence, therefore, should involve a determination of an individual's ability to make a particular decision at a particular time under particular circumstances. In the course of normal practice, therefore, assessment of competence will be an ongoing process.

In relation to minor and dependent adult clients, the assessment to be made is whether or not the individual is capable of giving informed consent to the proposed psychological service. The psychologist should determine if the client understands the following:

- the nature and purpose of the psychological service
- the risks and benefits of the psychological service

- the nature, purpose, risks, and benefits of alternatives to the psychological service

If the client does not understand all three of the above issues, a legally-recognized decision-maker (i.e., parent or guardian) should give—or withhold—consent.

SUMMARY

Informed consent means that the client understands whatever information is necessary to make a decision about undertaking psychological services and willingly agrees to them. Informed consent is required by our Code of Ethics and is based on the ethical principle of respect for the dignity of the individual. The central ingredients in informed consent are:

- the purpose and nature of the activity
- mutual responsibilities
- confidentiality protections and limitations
- likely benefits and risks
- alternatives
- the likely consequences of non-action
- the option to refuse or withdraw at any time, without prejudice
- over what period of time the consent applies
- how to rescind consent if desired

Freedom of consent is addressed by taking all reasonable steps to ensure that consent is not given under conditions of coercion, undue pressure, or undue reward, and respecting the right of persons to discontinue participation or service at any time. In situations with minor children or dependent adults, where the client is not competent to give consent, psychologists should secure the consent of a parent or guardian while incorporating the wishes and preferences of the non-competent person as much as possible.

1. Does a client have the right to be ignorant of risks associated with a psychological service if that person does not want to know? Explain.

2. Can there be truly informed consent in court-mandated situations? If so, explain how. If not, can a psychologist ethically provide services under such circumstances?

3. Under what circumstances would you allow an adolescent to consent to psychological services without parental knowledge or consent?

4. By law, people with severe mental disorders have the right to refuse treatment. How do you think we can best balance their right to autonomy against our obligation to help?

RECOMMENDED READING

Canadian Code of Ethics for Psychologists (Appendix A). Principle I: I.16–1.36; Principle III: III.14, III.32, III.33.

Crowhurst, B. & Dobson, K.S. (1993). Informed consent: Legal issues and applications to clinical practice. *Canadian Psychology, 34*, 329–43.

Hesson, K., Bakal, D., & Dobson, K.S. (1993). Legal and ethical issues concerning children's rights of consent. *Canadian Psychology, 34*, 317–28.

O'Neill, P. (1998). *Negotiating consent in psychotherapy.* New York: New York University Press.

Tymchuk, A.J. (1997). Informing for consent: Concepts and methods. *Canadian Psychology, 38*, 55–75.

Marital Secrets

You are a psychologist who provided marital counselling to a couple who is now separated. Many months after termination, you receive a telephone call from the husband asking you to testify at a child custody hearing. You contact his lawyer who informs you that you will be asked to verify that the wife had made admissions during counselling of numerous extramarital affairs. The husband's lawyer says he will argue that these affairs make her an unfit mother. You contact the wife and she insists that you maintain the confidentiality of the counselling sessions.

QUESTIONS FOR CONSIDERATION

1. What ethical values are in conflict in this situation?
2. What implications might your choice of action have for the profession as a whole?
3. Would it make a difference if you had never discussed confidentiality with your clients before or during counselling? Why or why not?
4. If you have deeply held beliefs in the sanctity of marriage and the wrongfulness of adultery, would this affect your choice of action? Why or why not?

SOURCE: From *Companion Manual to the Canadian Code of Ethics for Psychologists,* 3rd ed. (Sinclair & Pettifor, 2001).

6 ■ Confidentiality

THE CONFIDENTIAL RELATIONSHIP BETWEEN PSYCHOLOGIST AND client has long been regarded as one of the cornerstones of the professional relationship, second only to informed consent (see Chapter 5). The trust conveyed through promising and maintaining confidentiality is so critical that most psychological services may well be worthless without it. Most clients expect that almost everything they say in counselling will be held in strict confidence (Miller & Thelen, 1986; VandeCreek, Miars & Herzog, 1987). Certainly, without assurance of confidentiality many potential clients might never seek psychological services. People generally worry about being judged negatively for private thoughts and feelings about which they themselves feel uncomfortable or ashamed. Once services are undertaken, fear over lack of confidentiality might lead to incomplete disclosure of information, resulting in potentially ineffectual or compromised services.

VALUES UNDERLYING CONFIDENTIALITY

The importance of confidentiality is derived first from the ethical principle of respect for the dignity of persons in that it acknowledges that each person has the right to decide who has access to his or her private information. The upholding of the right to privacy is essential to maintaining individuality and selfhood. In many ways the loss of the power to make such decisions is the loss of one's true self. It is no coincidence that most forms of torture and imprisonment have loss of privacy as an essential cruelty. The Code of Ethics advises psychologists to:

> 1.43   Be careful not to relay information about colleagues, colleagues' clients, research participants, employees,

supervisees, students, trainees, and members of organizations, gained in the process of their activities as psychologists, that the psychologist has reason to believe is considered confidential by those persons, except as required or justified by law.

I.44   Clarify what measures will be taken to protect confidentiality, and what responsibilities family, group, and community members have for the protection of each other's confidentiality, when engaged in services to or research with individuals, families, groups, or communities.

Respecting the confidences of clients also reflects responsible caring because breaches of confidentiality usually leave clients feeling betrayed and, because psychological services are of such a personal and interpersonal nature, any benefit that clients may have accrued can be "undone" and any potential benefits will not be realized. Clients simply cannot benefit from psychological services in which they have lost faith. The Code of Ethics advises psychologists to:

II.30   Be acutely aware of the need for discretion in the recording and communication of information, in order that the information not be misinterpreted or misused to the detriment of others.

PRIVACY, PRIVILEGE, AND CONFIDENTIALITY

The ethics of confidentiality is complicated by common misunderstandings about some frequently used terms: *privacy*, *privilege*, and *confidentiality*. While these terms are conceptually related, they have quite distinct meanings and important differences.

Privacy

Privacy is the right of an individual to choose the time, circumstances, and extent of his or her personal presence, property, thoughts, feelings, or information being shared with or withheld from others. It is a basic human right guaranteed in the Charter of Rights and Freedoms (1982) and is considered essential to human dignity and freedom of self-determination. The concepts of privilege and confidentiality both grew out of the much broader concept of an individual's right to privacy.

Privilege

Privilege is a legal concept that addresses the right of an individual to withhold information from court or other legal proceedings. Privilege refers to *communications* occurring in specific *relationships* that are protected from disclosure in legal proceedings. Normally, anything relative and germane to the issue at hand in a court proceeding can and should be admitted as evidence.

It is important to clarify that communications in a psychologist-client relationship, except when the psychologist is the agent of a lawyer or during negotiations to settle litigation such as divorce mediation, is *not* privileged. This means that, potentially, anything disclosed by a client to a psychologist could be required to be disclosed in court. While other jurisdictions, such as most states in the United States and New Zealand, have granted an absolute privilege to some professions, the Supreme Court of Canada has held that privilege should be determined on a case by case basis. Perhaps equally important, privilege as a right belongs to the *client* not to the professional or to anyone else. If the client waives this privilege, the psychologist can be compelled to testify in court.

In most cases the justification for privilege is that the damages that would result from disclosure outweigh the damage done to the judicial process by not having access to the information. Arguments for privilege have tended to be justified on two wide bases. There is the utilitarian argument that to force disclosure would erode relationships that are deemed to be socially valuable. This is particularly pertinent to psychologists; most clients are treated on the basis that what they tell their psychologist will not be disclosed in a court of law, and there is a generally held belief that the possibility that this trust may be broken will be gravely detrimental to the professional relationship. More recently, however, claims of privilege have been justified in courts, not on such utilitarian grounds, but rather on broader social claims that some relationships are fundamental to human dignity and should be free from state interference, particularly those recognized in the Charter of Rights and Freedoms, a stance reassuringly consistent with our Code of Ethics.

Canadian case law (e.g., *R. v. Beharriell*, 1995) suggests that psychologists' records may be more easily afforded privilege than other records. Because every claim of privilege is judged on its own merits, however, records of a type that may have been ruled inadmissible in one case may be compellable in another. In the

Supreme Court of Canada case of *A.M. v. Ryan* (1997) the court held that substantial portions of a psychiatrist's records were compellable in a civil suit for sexual assault. Alternatively, in *M.(E.) v. Martinson* (1993), the importance of maintaining confidentiality of counselling records of treatment for sexual abuse, alcoholism, and drug addiction were found to outweigh any benefit they might have in establishing that the plaintiff's pain and suffering were not the result of the automobile accident which was the subject of the suit.

Psychotherapists' records in criminal sexual assault cases have received considerable attention from both the courts and the legislature. The Criminal Code sections 278.1 to 278.9 set out a series of guiding principles for when such records can be compelled by the defendant, as well as the mechanism for their inspection. Arguably, it may be that there is greater protection for the privacy of such records in criminal actions than in civil lawsuits.

Confidentiality

Confidentiality is a concept that refers to a professional standard of conduct not to disclose information about a client except under conditions agreed to by the client. In the context of ethics, it refers to an implied or explicit contract or promise on the part of the psychologist to keep private any information disclosed in the psychologist-client relationship. Although they are related concepts, confidentiality does not mean information is privileged. Violation of confidentiality may result in legal or professional sanctions against the psychologist.

With few exceptions (see below), every portion of the communications between psychologists and clients is considered confidential. A client may mention hobbies or food preferences in passing, and such information may not seem particularly private or embarrassing. If it is revealed to others, however, it is a violation of confidentiality. Remember that confidentiality belongs to the client; it is up to him or her to decide what will or will not be revealed and to whom. Even disclosure of insignificant material can feel like a violation.

LIMITS TO CONFIDENTIALITY

The ethics of the degree to which a psychologist should, if ever, violate a client's confidentiality are controversial. The reality, however, is that there are instances where the law requires it, or where the practicalities of maintaining confidentiality make it next to impossible to do so.

Mandatory child abuse reporting

All jurisdictions in Canada, with the exception of the Yukon, have legislation making it mandatory to report suspected child abuse. And all of these, with the exception of Saskatchewan, make the individual who fails to report vulnerable to criminal prosecution. The Code of Ethics supports this law in requiring that psychologists:

> I.45 Share confidential information with others only with the informed consent of those involved, or in a manner that the persons involved cannot be identified, except as required or justified by law, or in circumstances of actual or possible serious physical harm or death.

> II.39 Do everything reasonably possible to stop or offset the consequences of actions by others when these actions are likely to cause serious physical harm or death. This may include reporting to appropriate authorities (e.g., the police), an intended victim, or a family member or other support person who can intervene, and would be done even when a confidential relationship is involved.

And more fundamentally, the rights of any particular individual must sometimes give way to the rights of a more vulnerable individual, as articulated in the Values Statement of Principle I:

> Although psychologists have a responsibility to respect the dignity of all persons with whom they come in contact in their role as psychologists, the nature of their contract with society demands that their greatest responsibility be to those persons in the most vulnerable position.

Duty to protect third parties

The duty to protect third parties from a client's violent behaviour is established in law and may involve having to breach a confidential relationship. (See Chapter 3 for more detail.) It is important to keep in mind that a violation of confidentiality should only be considered under circumstances of possible serious physical harm or death. In a Nova Scotia case (*R. v. R. (K.A.)*, 1993) involving a physician who violated the confidentiality of a patient he had reason to believe was lying in a criminal case, the physician was suspended for three months by the College of Physicians and Surgeons for inappropriately violating confidentiality.

Client access to records

There has been some controversy and disagreement amongst professional writers on the subject of clients having access to a psychologist's professional records about them. The Canadian Supreme Court decision of *McInerney v. MacDonald* (1992), however, has clearly established that society expects psychologists to allow clients to have access to any and all information that health professionals have in their files that they have drawn upon to inform the provision of services. The court, however, notes that there is not an absolute right of access; a client may be refused access to the records if it can be established that doing so would result in harm either to the client or to a third party. Similar restrictions can be found in some legislation, including the Youth Criminal Justice Act.

While no codes of conduct for psychologists in any Canadian jurisdiction have been updated to reflect this decision, none of them expressly prohibit such action on the part of a psychologist. There may also be specific provincial or territorial legislation dealing with client access to institutional records that psychologists should be aware of. A good rule of thumb is to assume that any client may someday ask to see his or her records and that all who persist will ultimately be able to do so.

It is common practice to include material in client files that is never intended to be seen by anyone else. Speculative or impressionistic working notes that are meant to be incorporated into other documents, such as assessment reports or treatment summaries, are a common example. Psychologists should be aware that any written material might someday be disclosed and should take steps to avoid harm through mistaken impressions if taken out of context. It is prudent to make a regular practice of reviewing files and purging working notes so that one is not tempted to, or be accused of, selectively editing a particular file.

One area that remains problematic, however, is client access to original test protocols. The profession, to say nothing of the publishers of psychological tests, have an interest in keeping the content of most tests from the general public in order to maintain the utility of the tests. If people were able to obtain a copy of an intelligence test and study the correct answers, for example, it would not be possible to obtain a valid IQ score for them. Yet an individual requesting access to his or her records could not make any sense out of a test answer sheet without the test questions. Unfortunately this area has not been settled and it is best to proceed with caution. In many situations a thorough explanation of the issue will suffice to settle the matter. In other situations such as legal cases, however, the task is much more difficult and great effort may have to be expended in trying to maintain test integrity. Often it is possible to arrange to have the test materials given to another psychologist hired by one or more parties to the legal issue. Another strategy can be to refer the person making the request directly to the test publishers.

Third-party access to records

Psychologists should strive to ensure that no information collected or recorded about a client is revealed to anyone without the client's consent. There are, however, certain statutes that may compel the release of information with or without the client's consent, such as in worker's compensation cases. When clients submit a claim for benefits to an insurance company, they may not realize that in doing so they are also agreeing to allow the insurance company to obtain information from their psychologist such as diagnosis or type of service offered. The ethical concerns here are safeguarding clients' privacy and the potential for harm once information is no longer under the clients' control.

In addition to federal and provincial statutes that set out when disclosure of a client's records to a third party may take place, there have been a number of cases in Canada where release of information has resulted in allegations of negligence or libel and slander. In instances where the psychologist provides evidence in a court proceeding, the disclosure will likely be protected by the doctrine of "absolute privilege" which provides that a witness can testify in court without being liable (*Boychyn v. Abbey*, 2001). However if, for example, the psychologist provides comments to the press, such disclosure may be actionable (*R.G. v. Christison*, 1996).

When undertaking to provide services that are being paid for by a third party, psychologists should inform the potential client of the reasonably anticipated use that will be made of information collected and the limits on confidentiality before obtaining consent. In response to third-party requests, psychologists should make every reasonable effort to inform their clients of the request and to obtain their informed consent to release the information. In circumstances where the party requesting the information asserts his or her legal right to access without client consent, psychologists should obtain a legal opinion and make every effort to resolve the request in a manner that preserves the client's personal privacy.

Group and family therapy

The ethical responsibility to maintain clients' confidentiality does not change in group and family therapy. Psychologists still must not disclose to those who have no right to it the identity of or information revealed by clients. The fact that others are now privy to this information, however, does complicate matters considerably. It simply becomes impossible to guarantee that what is disclosed will not be revealed by others. The need to maintain confidentiality on the part of everyone in attendance should be stressed, but one has no real power to enforce this request. The best that can be done, therefore, is to discuss the issue openly and ensure that everyone understands the limitations.

Legally, the question of whether information revealed in group or family therapy can be regarded as confidential is an open question. When a person has revealed personal information in the presence of a third party, the courts have not tended to regard such information as confidential. Again, every effort should be made to explain these difficulties to clients so that they can make an informed decision about what to reveal or not to reveal in group or family therapy.

Court orders

In instances where a party to a lawsuit seeks disclosure of a psychologist's records, the duty may be onerous. First, an attempt should be made to determine whether the client opposes disclosure of the records. If the client does not and there are no other impediments to disclosure, such as requirements of the institution in which the psychologist is employed, then disclosure may be permissible. In such cases where the client will not consent, the party seeking the records should be instructed to make an application to court that will be provided to the parties in the lawsuit, the individual whose records are being sought (who will often be one of the parties), and the keeper of the records (the psychologist). At a hearing the seeker of the records will be required to establish that the records are likely relevant to an issue in the proceedings. Assuming that the records are those of a party to a lawsuit, the psychologist's involvement at the hearing may be minimal, usually being asked to swear an affidavit by the client as to the confidential nature of the records. Typically, the psychologist will not attend, nor be expected to have counsel of his or her own, although that is of course available. If an order is made, it may specify that the records be provided either to a party or to the court; in the latter instance a judge will review them to determine what should be disclosed.

If a psychologist is called to give evidence in a civil trial, it will usually be by means of a subpoena, which requires attendance with records. Again, the question of confidentiality arises if the client does not consent and in such circumstances the psychologist would be wise to engage the services of a lawyer.

In criminal proceedings there are no mechanisms for pre-trial disclosure of documents from third parties, so the psychologist will usually be called to trial by way of subpoena. Where the confidences are revealed in a forensic setting, however, such as assessing competency to stand trial or pre-sentence examinations, psychologists should advise the client that confidentiality is not present since the purpose of the evaluation is for the benefit of third parties.

Malpractice and discipline
If a client initiates a civil lawsuit claiming malpractice or a professional disciplinary complaint, the client should be informed that by doing so his or her right to confidentiality is waived. While psychologists might rightly have concerns as a profession that the possibility of revealing embarrassing confidential information may deter clients from exercising their right to legal remediation, psychologists also have the right to defend themselves. Procedurally, such concerns can be dealt with by conducting hearings in private and by excluding the public from courtrooms and sealing records involving sensitive testimony.

MINOR AND DEPENDENT CLIENTS

Psychologists providing services to minors are required to honour confidentiality in most of the same ways as with adults. Psychologists should not gossip about a minor client nor share client information with people other than the minor's parents or legal guardians without proper consent. The rationale for this position is the same as for adults: respect for the client's dignity and welfare. Children as young as six years of age are sensitive to issues of privacy, particularly with respect to being able to "be alone" (Wolfe, 1978). As children become older, they become more sensitive to control over their personal information (Wolfe, 1978).

The issue is more complicated than with adults, however, because minors are not fully autonomous individuals in the eyes of our society or their parents. Society has an interest in fostering the development of responsible citizens and in maintaining public safety. Likewise, parents have an interest in raising their children according to their own standards, which may be at odds with those of society. Even if the interests of the state and the parents are congruent, however, parents may not wish to allow others to access certain information about the child because to do so would reveal private information about the family.

In addition to this general interest in socializing their children, parents have a duty to protect their children from harm. This duty sometimes cannot be fulfilled without access to information that their children would prefer to keep from them. Given the nature of psychological services, psychologists often are privy to just such information.

If the minor's parents have given consent for their child to receive psychological services, what will and will not be disclosed should be clarified with them and the child. Legally, the parent or guardian who consents to services on the minor's behalf has the right to know the content of the child's service. Thus, a minor should not be promised that information will be kept from a parent who has legal custody.

If a child requests certain confidences, the degree to which confidentiality can be honoured is directly related to whether or not the child is determined to be a *mature minor* (see Chapter 5). If the minor's capacity is sufficient to warrant being treated as a mature minor, the parent or guardian no longer has the right of access to the child's confidential information. If not, the psychologist must still deal with the matter of limits to confidentiality. That is, the minor must be informed that his or her parents or guardians do have the right of access to all information that is revealed during the provision of services. Regardless of whether the minor client agrees to have information disclosed to a parent, the child should be informed—beforehand whenever possible—about what information will be shared. Ideally, the minor will be part of such conversations.

TECHNOLOGICAL THREATS TO CONFIDENTIALITY

With the expanding use of computers, the Internet, and other technologies to generate, store, retrieve, and transmit information, new threats to privacy are continually arising. Many psychologists, for example, keep their client records on computer. If this computer is connected to the Internet, files can be accessed by and distributed to others through a variety of means such as "worms" and "viruses," computer programs that access a computer, often via e-mail attachments. In one instance, a confidential disciplinary investigation report written by a psychologist about another psychologist was e-mailed to hundreds of people by a computer virus specifically programmed to look for the words *private* or *confidential* in documents stored on the user's computer. Problems can also arise in keeping communications between client and psychologist confidential. Clients or psychologists may have shared Internet access accounts that inadvertently allow other users to read their e-mails. E-mails can also be forwarded to unintended recipients through accidentally clicking the "reply all" button of one's e-mail software. These and other potential risks to confidentiality call for increased awareness on the part of psychologists.

Psychologists need to be aware of two important issues with regard to technology and confidentiality. First, do not take anything for granted with new technologies. A good rule of thumb is: *If you do not know how secure the technology is, do not use it.* Many psychologists keep a computer specifically for their client files that is not connected to the Internet or to e-mail. In any case, before using new technologies, experts should be consulted. Second, the same ethical principles and professional or legal standards apply to technologies as to non-technological situations. In fact, psychologists may well be held to a higher standard with new technologies than with old. It is the "psychological privacy" that is important, not the technological privacy that counts. That is, although in reality it is quite simple to open an envelope marked "confidential," there is a shared understanding of the risk and protections of doing so that gives us a sense of security and thereby constitutes acceptable professional practice. With new technologies, however, there is no shared understanding. In fact, most people probably have an exaggerated fear of privacy violations through Internet use and e-mail. Thus, even if one uses elaborate encryption software or other such means that, in reality, may provide greater privacy protection than an envelope, if confidentiality is breached clients are very likely to feel that they have been betrayed through lack of due diligence. Therefore, clients' understanding, familiarity, and comfort with any proposed technology used in the delivery of psychological services should discussed with them, and that technology should be used (or not) in accordance with the clients' wishes and comfort.

SUMMARY

Confidentiality is central to the professional psychological relationship. It is founded on the ethical principles of respect for the dignity of the individual, in that it acknowledges that each person has the right to decide who has access to his or her private information, and responsible caring, because breaches of confidentiality can "undo" the benefits of psychological services by betraying a client's trust. Psychologists should be aware of important limits to confidentiality: mandatory child abuse reporting; duty to protect third parties; client and third-party access to records, group, and family therapy; court orders; and malpractice and discipline. In situations with minor children or dependent adults, psychologists should discuss with the parent (or guardian) and the client what information will be kept within the professional relationship and what will be disclosed. Psychologists are responsible for addressing the threats to confidentiality that are being posed by new technologies for the storage and transmission of information.

1. Do you agree with the *Wenden* court's conclusion that our duty to protect others overrides our duty to maintain confidentiality? Why or why not? What ethical system does this decision represent?

2. Do you think that the fact that most child protection service agencies are overworked and far from perfect should affect your decision to report suspected child abuse? Explain.

3. Do you think that children should have the right to keep material confidential from their parents? Why or why not?

4. Do you think that confidentiality should be broken in the case of suicide? Why or why not? What ethical system does your position represent?

RECOMMENDED READING

Cameron, R. & Shepel, L. (1981). Strategies for preserving the confidentiality of psychological reports. *Canadian Psychology, 22*, 191–93.

Canadian Code of Ethics for Psychologists (Appendix A). Principle I: "I Values statement," I.37–I.45; Principle II: II.30, II.39.

Cram, S.J. & Dobson, K.S. (1993). Confidentiality: Ethical and legal aspects for Canadian psychologists. *Canadian Psychology, 34*, 347–63.

Schmid, D., Appelbaum, P.S., Roth, L.H., & Lidz, C. (1983). Confidentiality in psychiatry: A study of the patient's view. *Hospital and Community Psychiatry, 34*, 353–55.

Woody, R.H. (1999). Domestic violations of confidentiality. *Professional Psychology: Research and Practice, 30*, 607–10.

The Dating Game

You find one of your psychotherapy clients, who is approximately the same age as you, to be quite attractive. You notice that you think about this client outside of sessions. After eight sessions of career counselling you are discussing termination. In the last few minutes of your last scheduled session the client obliquely indicates an attraction toward you. You decide not to address the issue directly and services end satisfactorily. One year after termination you happen to meet the client at a social event. You easily strike up a very amicable conversation. The (now ex-)client indicates that the career change has been very fulfilling. The fact that both of you are unattached and not romantically involved with anyone also happens to come up in conversation. The possibility of the two of you meeting for lunch is raised.

QUESTIONS FOR CONSIDERATION

1. Is there any additional information you would want before deciding on a course of action in this situation? If so, what information? How would this information affect your decision?
2. Do you think that the romantic feelings experienced during therapy should have been addressed while therapy was occurring? What difference might it have made?
3. If you did pursue a relationship and it ended badly, what might be the professional implications for you? Would this affect your choice of action?
4. Are there ethical values in conflict in this situation? What other conflict might be present?

7 ■ Professional Boundaries

PROFESSIONAL BOUNDARIES ARE THE FRAMEWORK WITHIN WHICH
the psychologist-client relationship occurs and they define a set of
role expectations for the participants (Smith & Fitzpatrick, 1995).
Boundaries make the relationship professional, safe for the client,
and set the parameters within which psychological services are
delivered. Professional boundaries typically include service(s) to be
delivered, fees, frequency and duration of services, personal
disclosure, nature and extent of any physical contact, and the
general tone of the relationship.

IMPORTANCE OF BOUNDARIES

In any professional relationship there is an inherent power imbalance.
The psychologist's power relative to that of the client is derived
from the client's trust that the psychologist has the expertise to help
and the fact that the client is disclosing personal information that
would not normally be revealed. Given this power imbalance, clients
may find it difficult to negotiate boundary expectations or to defend
themselves against violations of boundary expectations that are not
in their best interest. As well, clients may be unaware of the need for
professional boundaries and may at times even initiate behaviour or
make requests that could constitute boundary violations. Therefore,
in order to protect the best interests of the client, psychologists are
ultimately responsible for managing boundary issues and are thus
accountable should problems related to boundaries occur. In essence,
proper professional boundaries provide a foundation for the client
to develop a trusting relationship so that personal issues can be
dealt with without fear of betrayal.

The primary concern in establishing and managing boundaries with each individual client must be the best interests of the client. As the professional in the relationship, the psychologist has the responsibility to ensure that he or she gains only the fee paid for the service (or salary), and perhaps a sense of professional satisfaction for a "job well done." Thus, it must be only the client's agenda that is furthered in the professional relationship. Psychologists should not meddle in the affairs of their clients that are outside of the professional agenda, nor share unsolicited personal opinions. Except for behaviours of a sexual nature or obvious conflict of interest activity, however, boundary expectations often are not clear-cut matters of right and wrong. Rather, the best course of action is dependent upon many factors, and decisions require careful thinking through of all the issues, always keeping in mind the best interests of the client.

ROLE BOUNDARIES AND DUAL RELATIONSHIPS

Dual relationships occur where the psychologist functions in one professional role and another significant role in relationship to the same person. The other significant role can be professional, authoritative, emotional, or some other. Examples include course instructor, work place supervisor, or friend. Dual relationships should be avoided because the expectations of one role may be incompatible or interfere with the other, resulting in harm to the client or the delivery of inferior services. The CPA Code of Ethics advises psychologists to:

III.31 Not exploit any relationship established as a psychologist to further personal, political, or business interests at the expense of the best interests of their clients, research participants, students, employers, or others. This includes, but is not limited to: soliciting clients of one's employing agency for private practice; taking advantage of trust or dependency to encourage or engage in sexual intimacies (e.g., with clients not included in Standard II.27), with clients' partners or relatives, with students or trainees not included in Standard II.28, or with research participants); taking advantage of trust or dependency to frighten clients into receiving services; misappropriating students' ideas, research or work; using the resources of one's employing institution for purposes not agreed to; giving or receiving kickbacks or bonuses for referrals; seeking or accepting loans or investments from clients; and, prejudicing others against a colleague for reasons of personal gain.

III.33 Avoid dual or multiple relationships (e.g., with clients, research participants, employees, supervisees, students, or trainees) and other situations that might present a conflict of interest or that might reduce their ability to be objective and unbiased in their determinations of what might be in the best interests of others.

III.34 Manage dual or multiple relationships that are unavoidable due to cultural norms or other circumstances in such a manner that bias, lack of objectivity, and risk of exploitation are minimized. This might include obtaining ongoing supervision or consultation for the duration of the dual or multiple relationship, or involving a third party in obtaining consent (e.g., approaching a client or employee about becoming a research participant).

III.35 Inform all parties, if a real or potential conflict of interest arises, of the need to resolve the situation in a manner that is consistent with Respect for the Dignity of Persons (Principle I) and Responsible Caring (Principle II), and take all reasonable steps to resolve the issue in such a manner.

As well, all jurisdictions in Canada that have adopted a code of conduct explicitly prohibit harmful dual relationships (see Chapter 2).

Overlapping relationships (Brown, 1991), where a psychologist has contact but no other significant professional, authoritative, or emotional role in relationship to the client, can be problematic but are not completely avoidable. Such overlapping relationships can occur in situations where, for example, the psychologist is of a particular religious or cultural affiliation and tends to practice within this community, is active in the gay and lesbian community and works with gay or lesbian clients, or has a child with a learning disability and is active in a local support association, and also does learning disability assessments. Overlapping relationships need to be managed on a case by case basis.

Psychologists should avoid relationships with their clients outside of the professional relationship where either they or their clients are in a position to give special favours, or to hold any type of power over the other. For example, psychologists should refrain from requesting favours from clients, such as babysitting, typing, or any other assistance that involves another relationship in addition to the primary professional relationship.

There are a number of areas in which maintaining professional role boundaries is challenging. Below are some of the more common areas that can present difficulties.

Giving or receiving gifts

Giving or receiving gifts of more than token value is contrary to professional standards because of the risk of changing the professional relationship. For example, a client who receives a gift from a psychologist could feel pressured to reciprocate to avoid receiving inferior care. Conversely, accepting a significant gift from a client risks altering the professional relationship and could leave the psychologist feeling pressured to reciprocate by offering "special" care. One must also be sensitive to cultural and individual differences when gifts are offered so that the client is not dishonoured. A frank but sensitive discussion of the client's motives can usually provide the necessary information to make an ethical decision. The decision should not be based upon a desire for the gift or to avoid discussing the client's motives, but on a judgment of whether the client would be more harmed than helped by the refusal.

Bartering and business relationships

The practice of bartering is problematic because it can create a harmful dual relationship. When bartering for services, for example, one takes on the role of the client's employer for the duration of the service. The professional contract is jeopardized in many of the same ways as in other dual relationships. The client's power to complain about working conditions or address problems in the service arrangement, for example, is limited. If the client expressed discontent with the barter, will he or she then worry that the psychologist will terminate professional services? In addition, the emotional role expectations can easily become confused when a client views his or her psychologist as an employer. Such confusion can reverse psychotherapeutic gains for the client. The psychologist's professional stance can also be compromised by the investment in the service the client is providing. If a client is bartering carpentry services for psychotherapy, for example, and the client completes therapy before the carpentry work is completed, the psychologist may feel tempted to prolong therapy. Conversely, the psychologist may feel tempted to foreshorten services if the carpentry is completed before the client recovers in therapy. Also, if the psychologist is not satisfied with the quality of the client's work, it can be very difficult to address one's concerns without compromising the professional relationship.

Social relationships

Generally, psychologists should avoid becoming friends with clients and should refrain from socializing with them. Although there are no explicit guidelines that prohibit friendships from developing once professional services have terminated, psychologists must use their best judgment in assessing the appropriateness for the individual client. Potential power imbalances may continue to exist and influence the client well past the termination of the formal professional relationship.

In the course of providing professional services, psychologists may, on occasion, engage in activities that resemble friendship, such as going on an outing with a child or adolescent, or attending a client's play, wedding, or special event. Such activities can be an important component of their services, particularly when working from a feminist perspective to minimize role expectations that entrench the power differential between themselves and their clients (Brabeck, 2000). In all cases, however, it remains their responsibility to ensure that the relationship remains professional and in the best interest of their clients.

Self-disclosure

Although in some circumstances self-disclosure may be professionally appropriate, psychologists need to be very careful in its application. A number of dangers exist in self-disclosure including shifting the focus from the needs of the client to the psychologist's needs or changing the relationship toward one that is more personal than professional. Such blurring of role expectations can confuse the client with respect to role expectations of the relationship and thereby degrade the quality of the professional services. As always, the primary question to be asked is, "Is my self-disclosure for the client's benefit?" Self-disclosure as instructive or illustrative can be a powerful therapeutic intervention when used judiciously, or it may be necessary to inform the client of any personal circumstances that may interrupt services, but self-disclosure should not involve details of current problems, personal fantasies, social activities, sexual practices, or financial circumstances (Smith & Fitzpatrick, 1995).

Rural practice
Psychologists in large urban centres have a much easier time avoiding dual relationships because of the large client pool from which to draw; they can more easily separate their workplace from their home life, and they can refer clients to other professionals in the same centre. Urban psychologists have the benefit of the relative anonymity of the large city so that overlapping relationships run little risk of harm.

Rural psychologists, by contrast, have dramatically different experiences. The pool of potential clients is much smaller, so turning away referrals can represent a very real financial hardship, and referral sources are limited and distant so that clients can be severely disadvantaged. And, unless one is willing to live as a hermit, overlapping relationships are a fact of life. Thus, the management of role boundaries and dual relationships is far more complex.

In a rural setting the potential for harm by turning away a client with whom we have another significant relationship must be weighed more heavily against the potential for harm resulting from the dual relationship. Jennings (1992) recommends that rural psychologists make a deep commitment to the core ethical values of the profession and develop a generous capacity for tolerating ambiguity in their relationships. On a more practical note, rural psychologists should make use of extensive, informed consent procedures (see Chapter 5), and consider providing briefer and less intense services to clients with whom they have more involved non-professional relationships (Jennings, 1992).

Forensic services
Some of the most troublesome professional role relationship conflicts, for both client and psychologist, occur in the forensic setting. Clients who are involved in legal proceedings typically have much at stake, from custody of their children to personal liberty.

Psychologists participating in such proceedings therefore run a high risk of having their client feel betrayed. Those specializing in forensic practice should be aware of the need for additional training beyond that required for entry into the profession (see Chapter 8), but even those who do not choose to practice in forensic settings can find themselves involved. The most common means by which this can occur is when serving in the role of therapist and being asked by the client to provide an opinion to the courts. Whereas the role of therapist is expected to be supportive, accepting, and empathic, when psychologists enter the legal arena in the role of an opinion-provider they have the legal system as a client and are expected to provide an opinion that is neutral, objective, and detached.

Psychologists must take extra care, therefore, to be clear about the nature of role expectations with clients when entering into a legal role. Potential problems should be discussed thoroughly ahead of time and often thereafter as events proceed or change.

Teaching

University and college faculty roles implicitly involve multiple role relationships with students. Professors can serve in the role of instructor, evaluator, advisor, research supervisor, mentor, and collaborator with the same student. Many programs also encourage informal, friendly interactions between professors and students. Although these multiple roles can be very beneficial for students, they can also become quite difficult for both parties, and role confusion is common (Rupert & Holmes, 1997). The potential for harm, apart from pure exploitation of the student arising out of the power imbalance with the professor, occurs when the professor's supportive and facilitative roles conflict with his or her evaluative role. The student's progress requires that struggles, concerns, and difficulties be shared with her or his instructor or supervisor in order that they can be addressed. If that same professor also has the role of evaluator, as most course instructors and many supervisors do, then they can be faced with a dilemma of helping the student improve and master the difficulties while also having to worry about the student's ultimate competence. Perhaps even more problematic, the student is faced with the dilemma of having to decide whether or not to expose his or her struggles and risk being evaluated negatively, or to keep them hidden and risk not attaining competence.

Friendly relationships can present similar problems for both professors and students in that the role expectations in a friendship are for a higher level of personal disclosure and reciprocity than are teaching relationships. Information revealed in a friendly relationship, as well as the expectation for friendly reciprocity, may then present complications leading to feelings of betrayal when decisions are made in the teaching relationship. Although rarely done, the best way to deal with these difficulties is to have different professors functioning in the different facilitative and evaluative roles.

SEXUAL BOUNDARIES

Sexual exploitation of clients by psychologists has come increasingly to the fore of public and professional consciousness. It has now become clear that for years professionals (and indeed many persons in authority) have taken advantage of their clients to further their own sexual and power needs with relative impunity. Fortunately, the courageous actions of increasing numbers of victims have forced the professional community and society at large to deal with the issue. The CPA Code of Ethics requires psychologists to:

II.27   Be acutely aware of the power relationship in therapy and, therefore, not encourage or engage in sexual intimacy with therapy clients, neither during therapy, nor for that period of time following therapy during which the power relationship reasonably could be expected to influence the client's personal decision making.

II.28   Not encourage or engage in sexual intimacy with students or trainees with whom the psychologist has an evaluative or other relationship of direct authority.

Physical sexual relations between a psychologist and a client, sexual touching, or behaviour or remarks of a sexual nature toward a client are professionally prohibited in all jurisdictions in Canada that have adopted a Code of Conduct (see Chapter 2). Under Canadian law sexual contact between a psychologist and his or her client is considered assault (see Chapter 3) whether the client gives consent or not.

There are **no** circumstances in which sexual activity between a psychologist and a client is acceptable. Sexual activity between a client and psychologist is always detrimental to the client's best interest, regardless of what rationalization or belief system a psychologist might choose to use to excuse it. Because of the unequal balance of power and influence inherent in a professional relationship, it is impossible for a client to give meaningful consent to any sexual involvement with his or her psychologist; client consent and willingness to participate in a personal relationship does not relieve psychologists of their duties and responsibilities for ethical conduct in this area. Failure to exercise responsibility for maintaining professional boundaries and allowing a sexual relationship to develop is an abuse of the power and trust which are central and vital to the psychologist-client relationship.

Prevalence
It is obviously difficult to get an exact figure for the incidence of psychologist-client sexual contact, but a reasonable estimate appears to be 10 percent for male psychologists and 2 percent for female psychologists, although these rates appear to be on the decline (Holroyd & Brodsky, 1977; Pope, 1990).

As one would expect because of the power imbalance between professor and student, sexual exploitation of students by professors does occur. Approximately 30 percent of female graduate students in psychology report having received sexual overtures (Glaser & Thorpe, 1986), with some 15 percent reporting having engaged in sexual activity with a professor (Glaser & Thorpe, 1986; Pope, Levinson, & Schover, 1979).

Causes
The majority of psychologists who sexually exploit their clients are males who are older than their female clients by more than a decade, experiencing personal problems such as loneliness or marital discord, and misinterpreting their client's overtures for support and acceptance as romantic or erotic, although a minority are calculating and predatory, or report being genuinely in love with their client (Bohoutsos, Holroyd, Lerman, Forer, & Greenberg, 1983).

Consequences
The vast majority of clients who have been sexually involved with their therapists report that the experience was exploitative and resulted in significant ill-effects as a result, including anger, mistrust of others, depression, and physical symptoms (Bohoutsos et al., 1983; Sonne, Meyer, Borys, & Marshall, 1985).

Physical contact

There are a variety of ways of using touch to communicate nurturing, understanding, and support, such as a pat on the back or shoulder, a hug, or a handshake. Such touch can, however, also be interpreted as sexual or intrusive, necessitating careful and sound professional judgment. Psychologists must be cautious and respectful when any physical contact is initiated, recognizing the diversity of individual and cultural norms with respect to touching, and cognizant that such behaviour may be misinterpreted. In Montreal where the dominant culture is French-Canadian, for example, kissing on both cheeks is a widely practiced greeting among friends, casual acquaintances, and, on occasion, between a psychologist and client (Smith & Fitzpatrick, 1995). Such a greeting would not be acceptable to most clients outside of Quebec, however.

Diagnostic and therapeutic work with children requires special consideration. Some agencies or institutions, for example, advise their staff to avoid any touching of children. In other settings, however, touching may be permitted, and this would ordinarily be open to public scrutiny. In working with children and considering the question of touching, one might ask, "Would I do this in the presence of my colleagues or this child's parents?" Again, considered professional judgment should prevail for the protection of both the psychologist and the client.

Some situations such as neuropsychological testing and biofeedback require touching the client. When such touch is necessary, it is important to obtain the client's fully informed consent prior to and throughout the procedure. If there is concern that a particular client may misinterpret one's actions, consider having someone else present in the session, an alternate treatment approach, or a referral to another practitioner.

Post-professional relationships

The issue of whether personal relationships with clients are acceptable after the professional relationship has ended is a difficult and controversial one. Some have argued that psychologists must never have a sexual relationship with a person who has ever been a client. This is in recognition of the fact that the influence the psychologist had while in the professional role never truly dissipates and so the power imbalance will always persist to some extent, leaving the (ex-)client susceptible to exploitation. Others have argued that this places a unreasonable limitation on our social lives, especially in rural settings, is disrespectful of the client's personal autonomy, and does not acknowledge the range of professional services psychologists provide and the corresponding degree of influence.

Professional standards strike a middle ground between these two views by requiring that psychologists refrain from sexual relationships with clients for at least two years after termination of professional services *or for as long as the client is vulnerable to the psychologist's influence*. This means that the onus is on psychologists to be sure that the professional contract was clearly terminated, the emotional component of the professional bond has dissipated (this applies particularly but not exclusively to psychotherapeutic services), and the psychologist's motives are not exploitative. Consultation with a trusted colleague is particularly indicated in such circumstances.

Avoiding sexual exploitation

There will be times when a psychologist will find him- or herself drawn toward a client or experience feelings of attraction to a client. Such feelings are normal and all too human, but should not be acted upon. It is vital that psychologists recognize these feelings as early as possible and take action to prevent the relationship from developing into something other than a professional one. If a client attempts to sexualize the relationship, the obligation is always on the psychologist not to reciprocate.

Before actual physical contact occurs there are often a number of changes in a psychologist's behaviour that alter the professional role boundaries toward more personal role expectations. Psychologists should be alert to such signs that suggest they may be starting to treat a particular client differently. These may include sharing personal problems with the client, offering to drive a client home, providing services in social rather than professional settings, not charging for services rendered, or scheduling appointments outside of regular hours, or when no one else is in the office.

The best way to maintain the appropriate boundaries in a professional relationship is through maintaining personal psychological health, awareness of potential problems, and clear communication. A psychologist's power over a client should not be underestimated. The psychologist should also remain aware that the client may experience touch, personal references, and sexual matters very differently due to a variety of factors including gender, cultural or religious background, or personal trauma such as childhood sexual abuse. Risky situations should be avoided and the proper boundaries of any professional relationship should be communicated clearly and early in the professional relationship. Ignoring established conventions that help to maintain the necessary professional boundaries can lead to boundary violations.

If a psychologist is having a problem with how he or she is treating or feeling about a client or how a client is feeling about the psychologist, assistance should be sought as soon as possible. If the client has been sexualizing the relationship, this should be documented, as should actions taken to address the situation. The psychologist is encouraged to talk to a trusted colleague or mentor, or seek professional help from a qualified practitioner in the psychological community or elsewhere.

Avoiding accusations

Although undoubtedly quite rare, false accusations of sexual misconduct against psychologists can occur. The following guidelines suggest approaches to avoid complaints:

- Respect cultural and individual differences regarding personal space and physical contact.
- Avoid making comments about a client's appearance, body, or clothing.
- Do not make sexualized or sexually demeaning comments to a client or about anyone else.
- Never criticize a client's sexual preference.
- Do not ask details of sexual history or activity unless directly related to the purpose of the consultation.
- Avoid "affectionate" behaviour with a client such as hugging or kissing.
- Never talk about your own sexual preferences, fantasies, problems, activities, or performance.
- Seek consultation regarding seductive clients and be assertive about your professional boundaries.

MAINTAINING BOUNDARIES

When faced with a situation in which the expectations of your professional role may be in conflict with those of another role, consideration of the following questions may be helpful when deciding how best to proceed.

- Is this in my client's best interest?
- Whose needs are being served?
- Will this have an impact on the service I am delivering?
- How would the client's family or significant other view this?
- How would I feel telling a colleague about this?
- Am I treating this client differently than other clients (e.g., appointment length, time of appointments, extent of personal disclosures)?
- Does this client mean something "special" to me?
- Does this action benefit me rather than the client?
- Am I comfortable in documenting my decision or behaviour in the client file?

If the psychologist's answer to any of these questions suggests that proceeding with a second role relationship with his or her client would not be in the client's best interest, the psychologist would be wise to delay the decision and engage in a thorough ethical decision-making process (see Chapter 4).

SUMMARY

Ethical psychological practice depends upon the psychologist always acting in the best interest of the client. In exchange for doing so the psychologist receives payment either from the client or in the form of a salary or third-party payment. When the psychologist has an additional personal or professional relationship with the client that includes additional expectations, either on the part of the client or the psychologist, the primary professional relationship can be jeopardized. Sexual involvement with a client is the most obvious and blatant form of boundary violation and is always unethical. It is also illegal in most instances. Sexual involvement with someone who was a client but is no longer is less straightforward, but is always unethical for as long as the client is vulnerable to exploitive influence by the psychologist.

DISCUSSION QUESTIONS

1. What is your opinion of the ethics of a psychologist having a sexual relationship with the parent of one of her or his child clients? Would sexual contact several months after termination of services affect your decision? Why or why not?
2. What is your appraisal of the two-year post-termination rule for sexual contact with clients? If you sat on the committee to rewrite the code of conduct, what position would you take?
3. Do you think the rule governing sexual contact with clients should be extended to include students? Why or why not?
4. What is your stance with respect to accepting gifts from clients?

RECOMMENDED READING

Canadian Code of Ethics for Psychologists (Appendix A). Principle II: II.27, II.28; Principle III: III.31–III.35.

Edelwich, J. & Brodsky, A. (1991). *Sexual dilemmas for the helping professions* (2nd ed.). New York: Brunner/Mazel.

Seto, M.C. (1995). Sex with therapy clients: Its prevalence, potential consequences and implications for psychologists. *Canadian Psychology, 34*, 70–86.

Woody, R.H. (1998). Bartering for psychological services. *Professional Psychology: Research and Practice, 29*, 174–78.

Yalom, I. (1996). *Lying on the couch.* New York: Basic.

MAINTAINING AND ENHANCING
COMPETENCE CASE STUDY

An Epiphany

You are a psychologist trained in individual psychotherapy with adults. Your father, with whom you were very close, died unexpectedly a few months ago. You found the shock very distressing and took two months away from practice to deal with it. Upon your return to practice you find that you have a new passion for therapy and a renewed sense of purpose. You realize that it is important that no family member should be angry and alienated from others in their family. You resolve to re-specialize in family therapy and to help clients make positive expressions of connection and love to their families because no one can be certain they will have another chance to restore the relationship.

QUESTIONS FOR CONSIDERATION

1. Do you think this example represents impaired practice? Incompetent practice? Why or why not?
2. If no clients ever complained about your practice, would this influence your answer to question number 1? Why or why not?
3. If a client sued you for malpractice, what grounds in law would they have?
4. What are your thoughts on the following point of view: "If every psychologist with 'issues' were to stop practising, there would be very few professional psychologists."

SOURCE: Adapted from *Casebook for ethics in counselling and psychotherapy: Standards, research, and emerging issues* (Welfel, 1998).

8 ■ Maintaining and Enhancing Competence

COMPETENCE IS THE CORNERSTONE OF PROFESSIONAL PRACTICE; clients seek services from a psychologist, as opposed to other non-professional helpers, because they expect them to be competent. Incompetent actions on the part of psychologists are unethical, unprofessional, and, under certain circumstances, grounds for malpractice because such actions are unlikely to be of benefit and likely to be harmful. A psychologist who is not competent to practice, therefore, should stop practicing. This is why competence is contained within the ethical principle of Responsible Caring in our Code of Ethics; being competent is central to protecting the welfare of recipients of psychological services. The Code encourages psychologists to:

II.6 Offer or carry out (without supervision) only those activities for which they have established their competence to carry them out to the benefit of others.

DEFINING COMPETENCE

Despite its central importance professionally, competence is not easily defined. At a very basic level, to be competent is to be able to do something (Jensen, 1979). Thus any definition must be based upon what psychologists actually do. To have declarative expertise (knowing what to do) is not the same as having procedural expertise (knowing how to do it). What quickly becomes apparent is that psychologists are engaged in a multitude of activities, so that professional competence must be considered within the context of the activity undertaken. Academic degrees, licensure, and credentials are not particularly useful indicators of competence (Koocher, 1979). Academic degrees recognize the successful completion of various course requirements, often with practical components, but seldom have any relationship to competent delivery of services. Licenses typically recognize that their holders have completed a minimum level of professional training, but they cannot guarantee that psychologists are competent to do everything their license permits them to do. Credentials rely on evidence that the individual has obtained a particular type of academic degree and holds a license to practice, and therefore add no new information as to the holder's competence.

Defining competence also has legal ramifications because society expects professionals to be competent, and remediation through the courts may be attempted if they do not meet these expectations. These expectations are functionally defined in the legal standard of matching the performance of an average fellow professional in good standing.

Competence is generally considered by most ethics scholars to be multidimensional and comprised of four major dimensions: *knowledge, skills, judgment,* and *diligence* (Norman, 1985; Overholser & Fine, 1990; Peterson & Bry, 1980). Some scholars include only knowledge, skills, and judgment, subsuming diligence under judgment. For our purposes we will discuss diligence and judgment separately.

Knowledge

Knowledge involves having absorbed and understood a body of information sufficient to understand and conceptualize the range of professional issues that psychologists can reasonably be expected to encounter. Knowledge is a necessary but not sufficient foundation for competence. In Canada basic knowledge is initially demonstrated by completing a graduate degree program in psychology, usually with a certain set of required courses, and by passing the Examination for Professional Practice in Psychology (see Chapter 2). Knowledge can be understood as covering a continuum from basic information that all psychologists should know, such as ethics, to specific knowledge necessary for specialized areas of practice, such as neuropsychology. Obviously, however, the knowledge base for a discipline is not static and continued study is considered necessary to maintain an adequate knowledge base. To be considered knowledgeable, a psychologist must stay current with developments in knowledge relevant to his or her practice. The CPA Code of Ethics encourages psychologists to:

II.9   Keep themselves up to date with a broad range of
        relevant knowledge, research methods, and techniques,
        and their impact on persons and society, through the
        reading of relevant literature, peer consultation, and
        continuing education activities, in order that their
        service or research activities and conclusions will
        benefit and not harm others.

Skill

Skill is the ability to apply knowledge effectively in actual practice. As with knowledge, skills cover a continuum from basic clinical skills of listening and interviewing, to technical proficiency for specific psychotherapeutic, assessment, or other professional procedures. Much more difficult to assess and even more difficult to instil, but also considered to be necessary, are personal skills such as self-awareness, tolerance for ambiguity, interpersonal sensitivity, and openness to exploring personal values, biases, and issues. It is generally accepted that supervised field experiences such as practica and internships are necessary to acquire the fundamental skills for the practice of psychology.

Judgment

Judgment involves knowing when to apply what knowledge and which skills under what circumstances. It also involves self-reflection on how one's own values, attitudes, experiences, and social context influence one's actions, interpretations, choices, and recommendations. Good judgment incorporates the intent of increasing the probability that activities will benefit and not harm the individuals, families, groups, and communities with whom psychologists have a professional relationship (Keith-Spiegel, 1977). Judgment is much harder to assess and is usually indirectly addressed during supervised experience. The CPA Code of Ethics encourages psychologists to:

II.8   Take immediate steps to obtain consultation or to
        refer a client to a colleague or other appropriate
        professional, whichever is more likely to result in
        providing the client with competent service, if it
        becomes apparent that a client's problems are
        beyond their competence.

II.10   Evaluate how their own experiences, attitudes, culture, beliefs, values, social context, individual differences, specific training, and stresses influence their interactions with others, and integrate this awareness into all efforts to benefit and not harm others.

Diligence

Diligence involves consistently attending to one's knowledge, skills, and judgment as they are applied in one's professional activities, and being careful to give priority to clients' needs over any other concerns. Diligence involves a willingness to work hard to provide the best service possible for each and every client, honestly evaluating one's own professional performance, and seeking additional training when appropriate. A diligent psychologist seeks out professional standards and guidelines that identify the knowledge, skills, and judgment essential to practice. Being diligent also incorporates self-awareness of any personal or situational circumstances that might diminish one's competence. The CPA Code of Ethics encourages psychologists to:

II.11   Seek appropriate help and/or discontinue scientific or professional activity for an appropriate period of time, if a physical or psychological condition reduces their ability to benefit and not harm others.

II.12   Engage in self-care activities that help to avoid conditions (e.g., burnout, addictions) that could result in impaired judgment and interfere with their ability to benefit and not harm others.

MAINTAINING COMPETENCE

The knowledge, skills, and judgment considered basic to being even minimally competent are not static. In constantly striving to deliver better services to clients, the average competence of the profession continues to rise over time. Psychologists must, therefore, continually keep abreast of new developments in the field in order to maintain competence. These new developments are typically knowledge in the form of new scientific and practice findings, and skills in the form of new intervention techniques and assessment procedures. But there are from time to time developments in professional judgment when what was once considered marginal but acceptable behaviour is no longer, such as some forms of dual relationships (see Chapter 7), and practice guidelines that are periodically produced by professional organizations (see Chapter 2).

Equally important is that psychologists as persons are not static. The profession is generally understood to be stressful. Psychotherapy is particularly so with its intense interpersonal, yet non-reciprocal, circumstance (Farber & Heifetz, 1982; Raquepaw & Miller, 1989). Psychologists also age, experience joy and suffering, form new relationships and end others, and generally change as people. Thus one's judgment also changes—often for the better, but sometimes for the worse (Thoreson, Miller & Krauskopf, 1989). Psychologists must also, therefore, stay abreast of their own personal changes and continually evaluate how these changes impact their competence.

What should become obvious from the above discussion is that there is no single way to maintain competence (Jensen, 1979). It is incumbent upon psychologists to monitor their practice continually relative to the state of the profession. When developments occur that "raise the bar" psychologists must assess the extent of the gap between their knowledge, skills, and judgment and take appropriate steps to upgrade. It is also necessary to monitor oneself continually as a person and professional, assess how any changes affect one's skill and judgment, and take appropriate steps to maintain competence. Among the activities to consider, in order from least to most extensive, are the following:

- Continuing education
- Peer consultation or supervision
- Formal consultation
- Formal supervision
- Additional training
- Retraining

ENHANCING COMPETENCE

For various reasons psychologists may wish to enhance or change their areas of practice or the psychological services that they offer. Psychologists may wish to offer additional services in assessment, intervention with individuals or groups, consultation, program development, or some other area. In that case, it is necessary to obtain whatever additional knowledge and skills are required to practice competently in the new area. One must become familiar with the standards of knowledge, skills, and judgment considered necessary for competent practice in the area one is considering expanding into, compare them with one's own, and develop a plan to acquire what is lacking. The means for achieving this goal are identical for those used to maintain competence, although of course one will typically have to undergo more extensive training. For example, if one were trained to provide psychotherapeutic services to adults and wanted to provide psychotherapeutic services to children, then retraining in basic and applied knowledge with respect to normal and abnormal development of children, as well as retraining in psychotherapeutic skills with children, would be necessary. This would necessitate coursework and supervised practice, which usually requires additional training under the auspices of postgraduate training institutions that offer acceptable training in those specialties. It is necessary to select a postgraduate institution that will provide the psychological education and training that is generally recognized as meeting standards of quality and appropriateness.

Another consideration in enhancing competence is whether doing so involves the acquisition of established and proven knowledge and skills, or more recent ones. With regard to the former, training or retraining is more straightforward and mainly has to do with acquiring expertise in the area of service. With more recently developed knowledge and skills, however, the issues are somewhat more complex. Training in new procedures and techniques is not simply the acquisition of new information, knowledge, methods, or techniques. The CPA Code of Ethics encourages psychologists to:

II.15 Carry out pilot studies to determine the effects of all new procedures and techniques that might carry more than minimal risk, before considering their use on a broader scale.

It is incumbent on psychologists, therefore, to ensure that any new approaches and procedures that are adopted will benefit and not harm clients. This requires critical evaluation of the new procedures and their incorporation into existing areas of expertise. Evaluation of the relevance and soundness of new procedures can be accomplished through several routes such as examining the scientific literature pertaining to the topic, consulting other professionals having expertise and experience in the area, and the exercise of critical judgment. Often all of these approaches are required for a thorough evaluation of new services to be offered before undertaking pilot studies.

AVOIDING IMPAIRMENT

Beyond becoming out of date relative to the state of the profession, psychologists must be vigilant with respect to becoming impaired. Because competence is based on performance, not ability, circumstances may arise whereby ability to apply knowledge, skills, and good judgment becomes impaired (Laliotis & Grayson, 1985). Reasons for this can be emotional such as burnout or distress, or cognitive such as substance abuse or dementia (Ackerley, Burnell, Holder, & Kurdek, 1988; Bram, 1995; Guy, Poelstra & Stark, 1989; Guy & Souder, 1986). Whatever the reason, one must do what one can to avoid becoming impaired, be vigilant with respect to impairment, and take appropriate steps to limit harm to others if one should become impaired (Mahoney, 1997).

The following suggestions should be considered to help avoid becoming impaired:

- Limit the scope and amount of your professional practice to what you can competently handle.
- Develop referral sources to whom you can send clients with problems you are not competent to handle.
- Develop and nurture a strong interpersonal support system.
- Develop a close, cooperative relationship with a group of peers to share the frustrations and excitement that surround your work.
- Take time to nurture your personal well-being.
- Stay involved in professional development activities.

If a psychologist should find him- or herself impaired for whatever reason, the following steps should be taken:

- Remove yourself from professional activities that could lead to harm to others, especially your clients.
- Arrange (or have someone else arrange) for your professional obligations to be met by terminating services or transferring responsibility to another psychologist.

- Seek appropriate help, including psychotherapy if indicated.
- Return to professional activity gradually as appropriate to the degree of impairment experienced.
- Review and revise your self-care practices.

AVOIDING MALPRACTICE

A review of Canadian case law suggests that malpractice claims against psychologists continue to be a rarity, albeit now becoming more common. Despite this happy thought, however, no one is immune from being named in a legal complaint. Psychologists deal with disturbed people struggling with sensitive issues and, under such circumstances, anything can happen. It is just plain smart to protect oneself from lawsuits and to be prepared in case one should happen. Beyond reasons of self-interest, psychologists do not practice in isolation of society and have an obligation to act in accordance with the standards of that society as reflected in the law (see Chapter 3). And, when one conducts one's practice in such a way as to avoid malpractice and the risk of being sued (which may or may not be warranted), one is striving to maintain the highest standards of the profession and thereby provide the highest standard of care to *all* clients served.

A professional liability claim, no matter how ill-founded, is a source of considerable stress to the defendant. The costs emotionally, and in time, cannot be understated. Once a claim is brought, the professional already has sustained a loss regardless of the ultimate outcome. One's approach, therefore, should be first to minimize the potential for claims. Professionals are more likely to have a claim brought against them by clients for whom they have just started to provide services. It is imperative then that during the initial visit, as much information as possible about the client should be obtained, including past history. Psychologists have an obligation to consult with previous caregivers, or at the very least review the client's records within a reasonable length of time of commencing services.

One's own clinical records should be as thorough as possible; by the time a claim is brought it is unlikely that many details of the case will be recalled. An action may be delayed considerably; in British Columbia the ultimate limitation period is thirty years, although most actions must be brought within six years. The value of clinical records is dependent upon their trustworthiness; notes taken during the visit or shortly thereafter will be given more weight than notes entered a week later. Significant statements by the client should be recorded, if possible, verbatim and indicated as such by quotation marks.

Also important is that, although the professional, and not the client, owns the clinical records, legislation in most jurisdictions allow clients access to their records (see Chapter 6). Such access, in circumstances where there is a claim or potential claim, should not be given without first consulting one's insurer or lawyer. Access to records can be refused, by way of court order, if it can be established that harm will come to the client if they are allowed to view their records. Such an order is, however, an exception to the rule. If access is allowed a copy should be provided and care taken to ensure that an untampered original is kept.

Typically, evidence at trial must meet the requirement of the hearsay rule such that the writer or speaker gives his or her own evidence in court and be subject to cross-examination. However, most jurisdictions allow the introduction of clinical records into evidence, even in the absence of the writer, provided they are made in the ordinary course of business, and at the time of the act recorded or shortly thereafter. An interesting question arises as to whether can be sued for libel for comments made in a consultation report or a clinical note provided to another practitioner. Most commentators believe that a successful lawsuit would be unlikely on that basis in Canada, although there is no case law on this point.

Consultation with other psychologists in difficult cases is both professionally and legally appropriate. Although mere concordance by another psychologist is not, in and of itself, evidence that there is no negligence, it does provide some evidence as to the reasonableness of the conduct. Such consultations, however, will be of little value unless a note is kept of the meeting or, ideally, a note prepared by the consulted psychologist.

Keeping lines of communication open not only with the client, but also with family (spouse, parent or guardian, etc.) if appropriate, may do more to avoid claims than any other precaution. Although there are no studies on the point, it would be reasonable to conjecture that a significant number of claims are brought, not necessarily by the client although his or her name may appear on the writ, but by the person who is responsible for their day to day support. A consistent feature in many of the claims is a statement by a plaintiff's witness that "I told them so...."

If you have knowledge of a potential claim, the first step will be to notify your insurer and then cooperate with the investigation. It is almost always inappropriate to apologize to the claimant; this gesture may later be construed as an admission of liability. A copy of your records will be requested, most likely by the lawyer appointed to represent you. You should try to provide as much material as possible and allow the lawyer to determine what is, and what is not, relevant to the case. The material you provide should not be altered or edited.

The standard you will be required to meet is not that of perfection; rather your conduct will be assessed on the standard of the reasonable psychologist, considering all the circumstances. If you hold yourself out as a specialist, the standard will be raised to that of a reasonable specialist in that area. In order to establish in court what the objective standard is, expert testimony will be introduced from other psychologists as to what is the approved practice. The reverse is, however, not necessarily true; the beginning psychologist is required to meet the standards of a reasonable psychologist of average experience. This is a legal standard based on the logic that the encouragement of beginners ought not outweigh the need to protect society.

If the unthinkable occurs and judgment is rendered against you, you must keep the finding in perspective. The court is not commenting on your general abilities as a practitioner, nor your competence in the future. A judgment for malpractice means nothing more than, based on the evidence before them, the court found that for the particular act or acts alleged your conduct did not meet the standard.

The following suggestions should be considered to help avoid malpractice:

- Present yourself honestly to your clients.
- Be especially cautious and careful in third-party situations.
- Document carefully and thoroughly.
- Consult with colleagues whenever in doubt and on
  a regular basis.
- Respond appropriately to signs of impairment as
  described above.
- Keep relationships with clients on a *strictly*
  professional level.

If you find yourself the defendant in a malpractice suit, the following steps should be taken:

- Stop being a service provider to the client suing you; respond defensively but not in a hostile manner.
- Do not contact the client; contact your lawyer immediately.
- Do not consult with others, especially anyone connected with your practice, and be discrete.
- Assemble all relevant documents and document all client contacts; show them only to your lawyer.
- Review literature relevant to your case.
- Be patient.

SUMMARY

Competence is comprised of four major components: *knowledge, skills, judgment,* and *diligence.* Psychologists should be fully trained and keep up-to-date personally and within their scope of practice so as to become and remain competent. Otherwise they should not be providing professional services. Psychologists should know their limits and refer cases they are not competent to handle. The science and profession of psychology is changing rapidly and it is important to be aware of new developments. Several avenues are open to psychologists for professional development to keep up with these changes. It is also their professional and ethical responsibility to evaluate the merits of new procedures and services for the best interests of their clients and profession. Psychologists should take steps to avoid becoming impaired and to limit harm to others should they become so. While lawsuits against psychologists are uncommon, they can avoid them by presenting themselves honestly to their clients, being especially cautious and careful in third-party situations, documenting carefully and thoroughly, consulting with colleagues on a regular basis, reducing or suspending their practice when in personal distress, and keeping relationships with clients on a strictly professional level.

1. Some say that the standards for practicing within the limits of one's competence are unreasonable for rural practitioners who must try to provide a wide range of services to a wide range of people. What do you think of this position?

2. Quite a few people enter the profession desiring to help others in response to their own histories of dealing with emotional pain. Do you think such a history is an advantage or disadvantage with respect to competence?

3. To what extent do you think that burnout is inevitable in the profession of psychology? Why or why not?

4. What self-care practices do you have in place to facilitate your continued personal well-being?

RECOMMENDED READING

Canadian Code of Ethics for Psychologists (Appendix A). Principle II: "Values statement," II.6–II.12.

Coster, J.S. & Schwebel, M. (1997). Well-functioning in professional psychologists. *Professional Psychology: Research and Practice, 28*, 5–13.

Farber, B. (1983). *Stress and burnout in the human service professions.* New York: Pergamon.

Grosch, W.N. & Olsen, D.C. (1994). *When helping starts to hurt: A new look at burnout among psychotherapists.* New York: W.W. Norton.

Maslach, C. (1982). *Burnout, the cost of caring.* Englewood Cliffs: Prentice-Hall.

Hearing Voices

A seventeen-year-old young man of First Nations heritage
has been referred to you by his school for an assessment
of his treatment needs. He has become increasingly
withdrawn and his academic performance has been
declining over the past year. He arrives with his parents
and, after discussing the purpose and nature of your
assessment, he states that he wants to have his parents
present. He reports hearing voices that are predominantly
benign and that he is unsure what the voices signify, but
that they do upset him. All indicators point toward an
incipient schizophrenic process. As you present your
opinion, the parents state that they do not want you
deliver this "bad news" to their son. They understand his
voices to be communications from his dead grandfather
who was a powerful healer. They fear that a pathological
understanding of his experience will sever the link with
his ancestral heritage.

QUESTIONS FOR CONSIDERATION

1. What is your initial reaction to this situation? How
   will this reaction need to be taken into account
   when responding to this situation?
2. What knowledge do you need to respond ethically
   to this situation?
3. What specialized skills do you need to respond
   ethically to this situation?
4. If some members of the family understood the
   boy's voices to be healthy, and some members
   understood them to be unhealthy, how would this
   affect your response?

9 ■ Providing Services Across Cultures

CANADA'S DEMOGRAPHIC LANDSCAPE IS CHANGING AT A RAPID PACE. Census figures tell us that persons long considered "minority" will become the numerical majority in the next few decades. The implications for the profession of psychology cannot be ignored. We will increasingly come into contact with clients from backgrounds quite different than our own and who may not share our world view about what constitutes desired behaviour and lifestyle. Psychology, along with most of the mental health professions, is only recently coming to grips with the impact that cultural diversity has on our practices. Minority persons tend to under-utilize psychological services, terminate services sooner, are generally given less preferential services, are encouraged to pursue less rewarding educational and vocational programs, and tend to be given more negative psychological evaluations than their majority counterparts (Sue, 2001). Indeed, commonly accepted professional services may be ineffective and even antagonistic to the desired outcomes of some culturally diverse clients. It is for this reason that psychologists who are not competent in providing services across cultures are at risk to be practicing unethically.

Culture refers to the set of shared meanings that form the structure of social interactions by providing members a set of standards and norms for acceptable behaviour (Fowers & Richardson, 1996). Note that the concept of culture applies to a broad range of groups who share a set of norms, and that assignment to a particular cultural group cannot be made without knowledge of the individual's subjective experience. While often associated with nationality, geographical ancestry, and religious affiliation, there are many other characteristics by which people identify themselves as belonging to a group, such as age, gender, sexual orientation, and physical abilities.

TABLE 9.1. The ADRESSING model: Nine cultural factors, associated minority group, and oppression

Cultural Factor	Minority Group	Oppression
Age	Older adults	Ageism
Disability	People with disabilities	Ableism
Religion	Religious minorities	Religious intolerance
Ethnic heritage	Ethnic minorities	Racism
Social status	People of lower status	Classism
Sexual orientation	Gay, lesbian, and other sexual minorities	Heterosexualism
Indigenous heritage	First Nations persons	Colonialism
National origin	Refugees and immigrants	Racism
Gender	Women	Sexism

SOURCE: From "Addressing the Complexities of Culture and Gender in Counseling," by P.A. Hayes, 1996, *Journal of Counseling and Development*, 332–38.

The idea of a *minority* refers to a culturally defined group that has suffered oppression by the dominant cultural group within a society. Such a group is typically, though not necessarily, numerically smaller than the dominant cultural group. Most importantly, minority status is a function of access to power within a society. Women, for example, are considered a minority even though they are numerically superior to men, due to their not having equal access to power in our society. Minority status is often loosely assigned by way of visible physical characteristics commonly associated with geographical ancestry, such as skin colour. The imprecision of such a grouping is usually further compounded by the use of the term *race* to categorize individuals who share common physical characteristics (Helms & Talleyrand, 1997) and to imply a vague concept of genetic lineage that, in reality, does not exist.

One systematic way to consider the interaction of culture and minority influences on professional practice is the ADRESSING model, presented in Table 9.1.

HAZARDS OF CROSS-CULTURAL PRACTICE

In order to understand the necessity of adopting a multicultural perspective in psychological practice, one must accept that not everyone has equal access to power in our society. In particular, many cultural groups have been subjected to oppression and mistreatment, and the prejudicial attitudes and behaviours that allow such violations to occur are far from extinct. Even psychologists, who as a profession obviously pride themselves on being fair and tolerant, may inadvertently perpetuate practices that disadvantage persons from minority groups. This is because they, just like every other member of a society, internalize the norms of behaviour of their culture. These norms provide information not only about how to behave in order to remain a part of the group, but also about who is not a part of the group. Potentially harmful errors of professional practice can result from either of these two information sources.

Cultural encapsulation

In order for cultural norms to be useful for guiding our behaviour and making sense of our world, we assume that others from our same cultural group share our circumstances, opportunities, and world view. Psychologists tend to be tolerant and accepting people and thus are particularly prone to assume that their theories and services are equally applicable to anyone regardless of cultural background. This mistaken assumption has been termed *cultural encapsulation* (Wrenn, 1962) and can render one ill-prepared to deal effectively with culturally diverse clients.

How many psychologists think about access to public transportation when choosing an office location, for example? Yet being inaccessible except by automobile is a disadvantage to persons who cannot afford to own a car. Such a decision would rarely, if ever, be the result of conscious discrimination. The effect is the same, however. Some multicultural scholars have even accused the mental health professions of engaging in cultural oppression by using harmful practices when working with culturally diverse clients. Again, such practices are rarely the result of conscious intentions, but are rather from "cultural blindness" that prevents psychologists from seeing the world as their minority clients see it. This blinding is perpetuated professionally by the belief that psychological practices are morally, ethically, and politically neutral (Ibrahim, 1996). When a minority client does not respond positively to psychological services, it is not uncommon to see the fault as residing in the client or, at best, in a poor match between the service and client. At worst, the client is viewed as pathological. What is typically not considered is a mismatch between the cultural world view inherent in the service and that of the client. Some psychotherapies, for example, pay relatively little attention to the client's personal history, while others rely on certain formulas of how certain historical or childhood events necessitate certain interventions. Still other therapies focus on rationality and the scientific method as the standard for mental health. And most forms of psychotherapy focus on the individual as the source of difficulties in life, the target for psychological interventions, and the standard by which psychologists judge success. These foci very much reflect the Euro-North American world view in which they were constructed, however, and can be at odds with the world views of other cultures.

Psychologists who strive to treat everyone the same, therefore, risk harming them because working with clients from other cultures may require differential approaches. Treating people differently is not necessarily preferential, especially when it provides for equal access and opportunity for psychological services.

Discrimination
The other function of cultural norms is to define who is and who is not a member of the group. If another person is categorized as not of the group then we do not assume that they share the same values as we do and we turn to whatever knowledge we possess about the group as a whole. That is, we can fall into the trap of not paying attention to individual characteristics of persons from culturally diverse groups. This manifests itself in the expectation that all persons from a culturally diverse group are different in the same way than persons from one's own culture. Sometimes these expectations are that persons of minority groups are inferior—the more common usage of the concept of discrimination—but it is not necessarily so. Some studies of psychotherapists have found that they have a "positive bias" in their assessment of culturally diverse clients (Jones, 1982).

Psychologists providing services to persons of First Nations ancestry, for example, may have very different expectations for their academic and career achievement than they would for someone of Euro-Canadian ancestry. Again, most psychologists would deny that they hold the belief that persons of First Nations ancestry are inferior, but the effect is the same as if it were intentional and, in many ways, is more difficult to confront. After all, who can argue that persons of First Nations ancestry are over-represented in Canadian prisons and under-represented in our universities and professions? Surely these facts should be properly considered when providing professional services, the argument goes. Such beliefs have been internalized from the negative messages and characterizations from the dominant Canadian culture and form part of psychologists' world view about culturally diverse persons. While generalizations about persons from a particular cultural group may be statistically accurate (or inaccurate; the argument is the same), failing to take proper account of individual differences and external influences is very likely to result in the provision of services that do not help—and could harm—clients.

A related caution is a failure to distinguish between characteristics that are the product of cultural influences and those that are the result of poverty or deprived status (Smith & Vasquez, 1985). Because members of minority groups do not have access to the same opportunities as members of the dominant cultural group, many live in poverty and struggle with its effects. Understanding their client's experience of these realities, which may be very different than their own, will help psychologists to provide fair and beneficial services.

In a culturally pluralistic society such as Canada, the process of acculturation, in which a person relinquishes the cultural norms of the culture in which they were raised and adopts the norms of another culture, has a particularly important influence on the provision of psychological services (Merali, 1999). Given that cultural membership is a subjective state, psychologists can best help and not harm their clients by understanding and respecting each individual's particular constellation of internalized cultural norms. Ultimately, understanding differences as active dynamics in the lives of their clients allows psychologists to tailor services individually, based upon their clients' needs and wishes, rather than reifying differences as indelible barriers.

A CRITIQUE OF THE CANADIAN CODE OF ETHICS FOR PSYCHOLOGISTS

As a profession, psychologists are still in the process of adopting ethical principles and standards that are multicultural in scope. Advocates of multiculturalism suggest that omission of such standards and failure to translate multicultural awareness into actual practice are inexcusable and represent a powerful statement of the low priority and lack of commitment psychologists as a profession give to cultural diversity. While that certainly is a harsh point of view, most commentators agree that psychologists could be doing more.

Codes of ethics have long contained standards relating to fairness and avoiding treating anyone, regardless of culture, unfairly or differently. In the current Code, *unjust discrimination* is defined as:

> Activities that are prejudicial or promote prejudice to persons because of their culture, nationality, ethnicity, colour, race, religion, sex, gender, marital status, sexual orientation, physical or mental abilities, age, socio-economic status, or any other preference or personal characteristic, condition, or status.

The ethical implications of this definition are elaborated in the Values Statement of Principle I, Respect for the Dignity of Persons:

> Psychologists acknowledge that all persons have a right to have their innate worth as human beings appreciated and that this worth is not dependent upon their culture, nationality, ethnicity, colour, race, religion, sex, gender, marital status, sexual orientation, physical or mental abilities, age, socio-economic status, or any other preference or personal characteristic, condition, or status.

And:

> All persons are entitled to benefit equally from the contributions of psychology and to equal quality in the processes, procedures, and services being conducted by psychologists, regardless of the person's characteristics, condition, or status. Although individual psychologists might specialize and direct their activities to particular populations, or might decline to engage in activities based on the limits of their competence or acknowledgment of problems in some relationships, psychologists must not exclude persons on a capricious or unjustly discriminatory basis.

There is some reference to the need for differential treatment:

> Psychologists recognize that, although all persons possess moral rights, the manner in which such rights are promoted, protected, and exercised varies across communities and cultures.

And:

> Psychologists recognize that as individual, family, group, or community vulnerabilities increase, or as the power of persons to control their environment or their lives decreases, psychologists have an increasing responsibility to seek ethical advice and to establish safeguards to protect the rights of the persons involved.

These statements appear in the Values Statement, with the following appearing as an ethical standard:

1.2   Not engage publicly (e.g., in public statements, presentations, research reports, or with clients) in degrading comments about others, including demeaning jokes based on such characteristics as culture, nationality, ethnicity, colour, race, religion, sex, gender, or sexual orientation.

Further statements prescribing avoidance of bias are contained under the Principle II, Responsible Caring:

II.10   Evaluate how their own experiences, attitudes, culture, beliefs, values, social context, individual differences, and stresses influence their interactions with others, and integrate this awareness into all efforts to benefit and not harm others.

And in Principle III, Integrity in Relationships, the following appears:

III.10   Evaluate how their personal experiences, attitudes, values, social context, individual differences, and stresses influence their activities and thinking, integrating this awareness into all attempts to be objective and unbiased in their research, service and other activities.

These standards, however, tend to perpetuate a culturally encapsulated fallacy of neutrality. Also, this non-discrimination approach does not take into account the need for differential services and the disadvantages faced by persons of cultural minorities. This issue is addressed to some extent under Principle II, Responsible Caring, by the following standard:

II.21   Strive to provide and/or obtain the best possible service for those needing and seeking psychological service. This may include, but is not limited to: selecting interventions that are relevant to the needs and characteristics of the client ... ; consulting with, or including in service delivery, persons relevant to the culture or belief systems of those served; [and] advocating on behalf of the client....

And, to a lesser extent, under Principle iv, Responsibility to Society:

iv.16 Convey respect for and abide by prevailing community mores, social customs, and cultural expectations in their scientific and professional activities, provided that this does not contravene any of the ethical principles of this Code.

Future revisions of the Code would benefit from attending to the fundamental value or world view conflicts that inevitably occur, but are so often missed, when providing services across cultures. Psychologists are advised to go beyond our Code of Ethics in order to fully achieve cross-cultural competence.

CROSS-CULTURAL COMPETENCE

Professional psychologists would do well to recognize that culture is central to their practice rather than ancillary. Both psychologists and clients are the carriers of their own cultures; each is a cultural being. In order to be prepared to provide competent services to clients who are different from themselves, psychologists should refer to the guidelines for non-discriminatory practice (Appendix C) and focus on four primary areas: *openness*, *awareness*, *knowledge*, and *services*.

Openness

First, we need to develop an *attitude of openness* toward other cultural views of the world and a tolerance for divergent views of right and wrong. When providing services to culturally diverse clients, psychologists need to be willing to accept that others will not have the same world view as they do; psychologists need to tolerate the discomfort they feel when they base their decisions on different standards than their own. This is, in essence, the ultimate expression of respect for their client's dignity as a person. Canadian psychologists are predominantly white-skinned, middle-class, secular males who are politically slightly left of centre. Most probably think of themselves as supportive of the struggles for women's and minority rights and opportunities. On the other hand, most believe that there should be clear boundaries between what they believe politically and religiously, and their professional behaviour and pronouncements. To be cross-culturally competent, however, psychologists need to move beyond this notion of a clear separation between the "objective" and "subjective" aspects of ourselves and consider actively welcoming different world views. While most psychologists will find such an attitude personally and professionally challenging, it can also be tremendously rewarding, in addition to being cross-culturally appropriate.

Awareness
Second, psychologists need to become more *aware of their cultural values, assumptions, and biases* about human behaviour; the lessons they learned from their own upbringing and culture. It can be surprisingly difficult to do. Some of the predominant values from a Euro-Canadian cultural background that are particularly relevant to psychological practice are an emphasis on the individual, an action-oriented approach to problem-solving, the Protestant work ethic, the scientific method, and rigid time schedules (Axelson, 1993). It is said that a fish has no sense of the concept of water, until on land. So, too, those of us who are members of the dominant culture typically have no more than a superficial appreciation of our culture until we open ourselves to the experience of being a member of a minority culture. This can be done in a number of ways. Living with members of a minority culture for a period of time is commonly prescribed. It can also be effective to live for a time in another geographical or national location where one's own culture is not the dominant one. In any case, an attitude of openness is necessary to learn the lessons of discrimination and to break out of our encapsulation.

Knowledge
Third, psychologists need to *gain knowledge of other cultures* and the biases, values, and assumptions about human behaviour arising out of the various diverse cultures within Canadian society. Such knowledge is particularly crucial when clients are struggling between the expectations of their cultural heritage and those of the dominant culture. Knowledge of the role of body language, tone of voice, eye contact, and confrontation, for example, can be critically important

when providing services to persons from a culture different from one's own. Obviously, it is not possible to become knowledgeable about *all* cultures one might ever come into professional contact with. But as an ethical psychologist one should strive to gain knowledge about the cultures of the clients one serves.

Services

Fourth, psychologists need to *develop culturally appropriate services.* Standard interventions or assessment methods may not sufficiently address the needs of persons from minority cultures. In particular, psychologists should be willing to involve support people from the client's cultural group and to make referrals based on the client's needs in relation to their culture when appropriate. This may involve referral to a psychologist or other professional who shares a common cultural identity with the client, or to a professional who is knowledgeable and skilled regarding the client's culture. It may also be appropriate to consult with an expert from the client's culture who may or may not be a psychologist.

SUMMARY

Ethical problems in professional service delivery may arise when there are differences of culture between psychologist and client. Cultural differences can be based on gender, language, nationality, ethnicity, ancestry, age, social status, religion, disability, or sexual orientation. The ethical significance is not the fact of difference in itself, but that the psychologist may fail to recognize the client's different world view or individuality, thereby failing to provide beneficial services or actually causing harm. Psychologists are cultural beings just like any other, but their professional status requires that they protect their clients' needs and safety by being more sensitive to cultural diversity in all its forms. Ethical psychologists should cultivate an attitude of openness to cultural diversity, make every effort to be aware of their own cultural world view, gain knowledge of their clients' culture(s), and develop culturally appropriate services.

1. In some societies the norms differ dramatically from what are considered universal human rights. For example, in some countries girls and women are currently denied education. Can psychologists provide services respectfully with clients from such cultures and still honour those values?

2. Should unintentional acts of racial discrimination be dealt with by disciplinary bodies differently than intentional acts? If so, identify the differences you think are important.

3. What do you think of the relative importance of life experiences versus professional training in order for psychologists to be cross-culturally competent?

4. What do you think of the ethics of restricting one's practice to only providing services to clients of the same cultural background as yourself, such as lesbians, white men, First Nations persons, or middle-class professionals?

RECOMMENDED READING

Canadian Code of Ethics for Psychologists (Appendix A). Principle I: "Values statement," I.2, I.9–I.11; Principle II: II.10, II.14, ii21; Principle III: III.10; Principle IV: IV.15, IV.16.

Merali, N. (1999). Resolution of value conflicts in multicultural counselling. *Canadian Journal of Counselling, 33*, 28–36.

Merali, N. (2002). Culturally informed ethical decision making in situations of suspected child abuse. *Canadian Journal of Counselling, 36*, 233–44.

Pettifor, J.L. (2001). Are professional codes of ethics relevant for multicultural counselling? *Canadian Journal of Counselling, 35*, 26–35.

Sue, D.W. (2001). Multidimensional facets of cultural competence. *The Counseling Psychologist, 29*, 790–821.

The Disruptive Student

You have been asked to assess an eight-year-old student who is being very disruptive in class. He has been making loud, angry outbursts, destroying other students' property, and once attempted to start a fire in a wastebasket. Other students are being deprived of educational opportunities and are at some risk of physical harm.

Upon assessment, there is no question that the boy has individual needs that can only be addressed by services that cannot be implemented in his regular classroom.

A special education class that would be able to provide appropriate services is full, however, with a long waiting list. Services are available at a nearby private facility, but are very expensive. If the school were to refer the boy they would be obligated to provide funding according to provincial regulation. Doing so would thereby deplete the school's entire budget for such services.

QUESTIONS FOR CONSIDERATION

1. What are your professional obligations with respect to the eight-year-old student?

2. What are your professional obligations with respect to the other students in his classroom?

3. On what basis would you weigh your obligations to the eight-year-old student against those of the other students in his classroom?

4. If you happened to be a member of the advisory committee of the school board, and knew that the special education class was scheduled to be discontinued, how would this affect your choice of action?

10 ■ Social Justice and Responsibility

THE CONCEPT OF SOCIAL JUSTICE IS AS OLD AS CIVILIZATION ITSELF and was the subject of serious consideration by the ancient Greek philosophers Plato and Aristotle. Social justice is about ensuring that all people have access to resources and are treated fairly regardless of their status within society. Psychology functions as a profession within the context of society. Indeed, it can be said that the profession of psychology exists in large part because it is recognized by our society. Professional psychologists, therefore, have responsibilities to the societies in which they live and work and by extension to the welfare of all members of those societies. Traditionally, the expectations of psychology as a science and a profession are that its members will increase knowledge and promote the welfare of all human beings. Social justice, however, would argue against this narrow expectation and in favour of confronting disadvantage in all its forms in our society. A just society would be one where human rights and liberties are safeguarded, material resources are equally distributed, and there is greater public involvement in societal decision making. If psychologists are truly concerned with human welfare, such considerations ought to be a part of their professional identity. Concern for the betterment of society and social systems for the benefit of all individuals are the realm of social responsibility ethics.

One of the most unique features of the Canadian Code of Ethics for Psychologists is setting out responsibility to society as a core ethical principle, and the Values Statement is worth quoting at length:

> Psychologists will do whatever they can to ensure that
> psychological knowledge, when used in the development
> of social structures and policies, will be used for beneficial
> purposes, and that the discipline's own structures and

policies will support those beneficial purposes....
If psychological knowledge or structures are used against
these purposes, psychologists have an ethical responsibility
to try to draw attention to and correct the misuse.

Some particular standards are also important to acknowledge
whereby psychologists are expected to:

IV.6 Participate in the process of critical self-evaluation
of the discipline's place in society, and in the
development and implementation of structures
and procedures that help the discipline to contribute
to beneficial societal functioning and changes.

IV.22 Speak out, in a manner consistent with the four
principles of this Code, if they possess expert
knowledge that bears on important societal issues
being studied or discussed.

IV.29 Speak out and/or act, in a manner consistent with the
four principles of this Code, if the policies, practices,
laws, or regulations of the social structure within
which they work seriously ignore or contradict any
of the principles of this Code.

Whereas the Code seems to differentiate social responsibility from
respect for individuals and make it a subordinate consideration
(Clark, 1993), Principle I contains much that is representative of the
foundational ethical principle of justice. The values statement of
Principle I articulates the belief that:

all persons have a right to have their innate worth as
human beings appreciated and that this worth is not
dependent upon their culture, nationality, ethnicity, colour,
race, religion, sex, gender, marital status, sexual
orientation, physical or mental abilities, age, socio-
economic status, or any other preference or personal
characteristic, condition, or status.

And that:

all persons are entitled to benefit equally from the
contributions of psychology and to equal quality in the
processes, procedures, and services being conducted by
psychologists, regardless of the person's characteristics,
condition, or status.

Principle IV, Responsibility to Society, although presented as subordinate to the other three ethical principles, is the only principle to make explicit reference to human welfare beyond the level of the individual. Psychological knowledge is to be used for beneficial social purposes, as conceptualized in terms of respect for the dignity of persons, responsible caring, and integrity in relationships. Psychologists therefore have an ethical obligation to try to correct any misuse of psychological knowledge against these purposes, but are also expected to respect social structures and avoid unwarranted disruptions of them. Actions intended to produce social change are to be carried out primarily through education, although criticism and advocacy of rapid change may be justified when social systems oppose fundamental human rights.

So the responsibilities of psychologists toward society can be understood as twofold: Concern for all persons as individuals (social justice) and concern for social betterment (social responsibility).

SOCIAL JUSTICE ISSUES IN PSYCHOLOGICAL PRACTICE

Traditionally, the issue of social justice has been thought of as the concern of policy planners and politicians. Indeed, the Code states:

> Although [correcting misuse of psychological knowledge] is a collective responsibility, those psychologists having direct involvement in the structures of the discipline, in social development, or in the theoretical or research data base that is being used (e.g., through research, expert testimony, or policy advice) have the greatest responsibility to act. Other psychologists must decide for themselves the most appropriate and beneficial use of their time and talents to help meet this collective responsibility.

Yet "front line" psychologists providing services to clients are in the position not only to listen and affirm, but also to help with the interpretation of private troubles of individuals as justice issues. Also, psychologists are often faced with decisions involving demand for psychological and other mental health services exceeding resources. Deciding how they should be distributed in a fair and equitable manner is a social justice issue.

The basic ethical requirement of social justice can be stated: *Equals must be treated as equals, and unequals must be treated as unequals.* This means that persons who are equal in whatever aspects that are relevant to a decision must be treated as equals. This rarely helps much in decision making because it is often difficult to agree on what aspects are relevant to deciding how to distribute resources. Potentially relevant aspects are: need, effort, contribution, merit, equal share, and free-market exchanges. What we need is a systematic framework for making decisions about what aspects are relevant to particular circumstances. In Canada we have historically adopted the principle that everyone has the right to equitable and just access to health care (Kluge, 1992). The framework for realizing this principle is that of *fair opportunity* (Beauchamp & Childress, 2001; Daniels, 1985; Rawls, 1971). Fair opportunity says that no persons should receive services on the basis of undeserved advantageous attributes (because no persons are responsible for having these attributes) and that no persons should be denied services on the basis of undeserved disadvantageous attributes (because they similarly are not responsible for having these attributes).

Take, for example, the issue of access to educational opportunities. Imagine that an educational system offers a high-quality education to all children with basic abilities, regardless of such attributes as gender or minority status, but not to children with attributes that interfere with the realization of their basic abilities. Such a system would be unjust because children are not responsible for their disadvantageous attributes. The fair opportunity rule leads to the conclusion that they should receive an education suitable to their needs and opportunities, even if it costs more.

The issue is made even more difficult, however, when one attempts to allocate services within a fixed budget. Canadian society has decided that all children should receive educational services, but does not allocate unlimited finances to pay for unlimited services. In the normal course of allocating limited services to individuals, therefore, likelihood of success if the service were to be provided to the particular individual(s) is considered first, followed by "first come, first served" when likelihood of success is roughly equal for eligible recipients (Beauchamp & Childress, 2001). In this way deontological (egalitarian) principles are balanced with teleological (utilitarian) considerations.

SOCIAL RESPONSIBILITY

Concern about social betterment is grounded in respect for the rights, dignity, and worth of individuals. Certainly the reduction of human suffering and furtherance of human rights are the basis of psychology's concern about society in general. But social responsibility goes beyond the particular ethical obligations owed to individuals arising out of psychologists' professional relationships, to include ethical obligations to all individuals within a society.

One might well argue that much of the misery that psychologists address is the product of the exploitation and misuse of human beings. Many of the circumstances that prompt individuals to seek help from psychologists can be understood as being the direct or indirect consequence of oppression and unjust social, economic, and political institutions. The principle of Responsibility to Society encourages psychologists to be concerned for the welfare of all human beings in society. It follows that psychologists' commitment to the welfare of others can be understood as bringing with it a responsibility to change social systems. Because there are multiple avenues for social action, psychologists may choose for themselves the most appropriate and beneficial use of their time and talents to help meet this collective responsibility. Knowledge may be used to influence social policy. Public education, advocacy, or lobbying are also appropriate.

If social policy and societal attitudes seriously ignore or violate the ethical principles of autonomy, beneficence, nonmaleficence, and fidelity to the harm of members of our society, then psychologists have a responsibility to advocate for change to occur as quickly as possible. There is social injustice when segments of our society are devalued or oppressed. To the extent that individuals and groups without power suffer oppression in our imperfect society, psychologists have an ethical responsibility to use their knowledge and power to contribute to social change. One can easily see that social value considerations pervade all of our work, and it will ever be thus. The choice is whether or not to engage openly in socially responsible activities.

A CALL TO ACTION

To a large extent, psychologists epitomize the goals of the progressive social reform movement of promoting the well-being of all people. The reality, however, is that most psychologists do not spend much time thinking about such things, and even less time taking action to improve society. Terms such as *activist, advocacy, social action,* and *change agent* are far from prominent in the psychological literature. Psychologists are typically not trained to try to change the circumstances causing various social problems or alleviating the effects. They tend to focus on the individual and direct their activities at individual problems. Such an approach tends to be a passive, reactive one in which clients are assisted in taking responsibility for helping themselves. Therefore, the solutions to problems, choices, and challenges confronting their clients are viewed as being within the clients' grasp if they can figure out how to solve the problems, make the choices, and meet the challenges successfully. But such an approach may be too passive and uninvolved, and many clients are in situations in which they cannot achieve their goals or resolve their problems through their own self-directed efforts.

ETHICAL CONFLICTS IN SOCIAL ACTIVISM

Most would agree that the broad goal of improving our social systems for the benefit of all members of society is desirable. The role that psychology as a profession should play in bringing about such improvements, however, enjoys much less agreement. The role that an individual psychologist might play in particular circumstances arouses downright dissension. In fact, responding to social responsibility ethics in particular cases that involve individuals are very likely to give rise to ethical conflict.

While it may be desirable for the profession to advocate openly for social change, when enacted by individual psychologists it appears very much like bias (Brown, 1997). In general, psychologists are expected to assume an "objective" stance in relation to the people to whom they provide services. This means that psychologists are expected to simply report their findings as they are—without bias, distortion, or hidden agenda. If psychologists make their social advocacy agenda explicit, therefore, they need to be aware that their opinions are likely to be perceived as biased and may not be considered by the very persons whose decisions they hope to influence. Psychologists would also be very unlikely to continue to receive referrals for such services and their opinions would therefore be excluded from future decisions. Professionals whose opinions are uninformed by social responsibility ethics or whose opinions support existing systems will then be more likely to have input into decisions about individuals. Thus, psychologists are placed in a dilemma of either covertly addressing particular social issues as they affect individuals and thereby violating their ethical obligations to avoid misrepresentation and deception, or abandoning their social responsibility ethics. And ultimately, a failure to be forthcoming about one's social policy position, no matter how valid and noble it may be, is to risk the loss of role integrity (Clark, 1993; O'Neill, 1989), with all of the associated negative consequences for the psychologist, the profession, and the individuals involved.

When psychologists have undertaken a professional role to provide services to individuals, therefore, they need to carefully balance the risks associated with advocacy for particular social values or changes with the missed opportunity for social betterment. Psychologists must always work to ensure that the individuals they come in contact with are treated justly by the systems psychologists are a part of. In so doing, psychologists should be open about their social values and act in accordance with them in all of their professional activities. When those systems are unjust, psychologists should seek change at the system level.

The following questions may assist you when considering social action in individual cases:

- Is my knowledge of the matter sufficiently complete and accurate?
- To what extent is this a case of individual rights as opposed to an unjust system?
- Will I be violating any implicit or explicit agreements by taking social action?
- Will I be violating any implicit or explicit agreements by *not* taking social action?
- What way has the best chance of promoting positive change while still being ethical?
- What can I realistically expect to achieve by taking social action in this particular matter?
- Am I willing to make the personal and professional sacrifices that will likely be necessary if I take action?

SUMMARY

In this chapter the ethical values of *social justice* and *social responsibility* are defined and discussed. Social justice is concerned with the well being of individuals by assuring that all have equal access to psychological and other needed services. Social responsibility is concerned with the betterment of society and social systems for the benefit of all individuals. Obligations and dilemmas arising out of these values can occur at the level of the individuals and the social systems with which psychologists interact. The ethical conflicts inherent in social advocacy are between social responsibility and professional role integrity. If a just system is being applied unjustly, psychologists should advocate on behalf of their clients. If a system is unjust, psychologists have a responsibility to take action at the systems level.

DISCUSSION QUESTIONS

1. Do you think that psychological services are fairly distributed among all Canadians?
2. What do you think is the basic level of psychological health that all members of society are entitled to? How would such a level be determined?
3. To what extent do you think psychologists have an obligation to promote social change?
4. Should efforts to make social change be made if doing so would violate other ethical principles? If doing so would violate the law? What ethical system does your answer reflect?

RECOMMENDED READING

Canadian Code of Ethics for Psychologists (Appendix A). Principle I: "Values statement," I.7, I.12, I.13; Principle II: II.38, II.43; Principle IV: "Values statement," IV.6, IV.20–IV.29.

O'Neill, P. (1989). Responsible to whom? Responsible for what? Some ethical issues in community intervention. *American Journal of Community Psychology, 17,* 323–41.

Pettifor, J.L. (1996). Ethics: Virtue and politics in the science and practice of psychology. *Canadian Psychology, 37,* 1–12.

Prilleltensky, I. (1990). Enhancing the social ethics of psychology: Toward a psychology at the service of social change. *Canadian Psychology, 31,* 310–19.

11 ■ The Ethical Psychologist

FEW WOULD DISAGREE THAT ETHICS OUGHT TO BE TAUGHT. NOT everyone agrees that ethics can be learned. In the Introduction we argued that in order to be an ethical psychologist one needs awareness of situations and circumstances in which ethical reasoning is required, knowledge of ethical, professional, and legal standards, and skills to arrive at an ethically justifiable decision. We also conceded that the development of professional ethical awareness is a life-long process and that professional training alone may not be enough. It may be that training, no matter how targeted at ethical knowledge and reasoning, will not ultimately inspire ethical behaviour. In the end, even the most aware, knowledgeable, and skilled psychologist may choose to act unethically. This does not mean that codes and laws are useless. It does mean that rules are insufficient to ensure ethical practice.

Most psychologists subscribe to the basic ethical principles and rules of their profession. In like manner, most support and obey the law and generally accept the need for societal rules to govern human conduct. But few do so blindly or without question. Quite frequently, personal independence is asserted by choosing to ignore a rule, disobey a law, or violate a principle because it seems that the matter does not apply to oneself or is insignificant. Or psychologists may disobey a rule, law, or principle because they believe that it is wrong. In other words, they make a free choice, for or against a law or a principle and for or against ethical behaviour. This choice is an individual matter and beyond the reach of any person, group, or power.

Similarly, no matter how sophisticated professional codes and standards become, there will always be practitioners who consciously breach or challenge the limits of ethical behaviour. Moreover, it is unlikely that unethical and illegal practices will be significantly curtailed through more external controls. Scoundrels can still hold proper credentials and meet all legal qualifications for entry into the profession.

Each of us is responsible for our own behaviour. Principles and values provide a common vocabulary to make ethical decisions and to use when thinking through difficult situations, but we must decide how we will respond in a particular situation. Often people may know ethical rules and standards and in most cases adhere to them, sometimes reluctantly, but seem to lack a depth of understanding of or awkwardness about what it means to be ethical. When we have internalized ethical principles and values, on the other hand, we act ethically because it feels right. Our actions reflect a state of coherent integration between all aspects of ourselves—emotions, cognitions, and behaviours. An absence of integration is characterized by hypocrisy or insincerity.

How then to attain such a state of being? Integrity is engendered through consistently striving to be ethical in every situation. It cannot merely be gained as knowledge; it must be practiced. Therefore, we encourage you to be mindful of your ethical self and the ethics of your actions in all of your activities.

There is one important potential pitfall of integrity—becoming overly rigid in upholding ethical values. Thus, integrity must be moderated by wisdom. Wisdom is intellect in the service of compassion. Compassion is the realization that others are as important as ourselves and not behaving purely out of self-interest. Wise psychologiests draw upon their knowledge, skills, and judgment to further the welfare of others out of a deep respect for their suffering and innate worth. In the words of Aldous Huxley:

> It's a bit embarrassing to have been concerned with the
> human problem all one's life and find at the end that one
> has no more to offer than, 'Try to be a little kinder.'

Compassion helps psychologists to avoid the potential pitfall of integrity—becoming overly rigid in upholding their ethical values. And bringing to bear their intellect can keep their (com)passion from overwhelming their judgment.

So, can ethics be learned? Not entirely. We do encourage you to learn the material contained in this book. Think about it. Struggle with it. Debate it. Incorporate it into your way of making sense of the world. And then choose to apply it or not. Ultimately, it is the choice to act ethically that is the greatest lesson.

Canadian Code of Ethics for Psychologists

Third Edition

PREAMBLE

Introduction

Every discipline that has relatively autonomous control over its entry requirements, training, development of knowledge, standards, methods, and practices does so only within the context of a contract with the society in which it functions. This social contract is based on attitudes of mutual respect and trust, with society granting support for the autonomy of a discipline in exchange for a commitment by the discipline to do everything it can to assure that its members act ethically in conducting the affairs of the discipline within society; in particular, a commitment to try to assure that each member will place the welfare of the society and individual members of that society above the welfare of the discipline and its own members. By virtue of this social contract, psychologists have a higher duty of care to members of society than the general duty of care that all members of society have to each other.

The Canadian Psychological Association recognizes its responsibility to help assure ethical behaviour and attitudes on the part of psychologists. Attempts to assure ethical behaviour and attitudes include articulating ethical principles, values, and standards; promoting those principles, values, and standards through education, peer modelling, and consultation; developing and implementing methods to help psychologists monitor the ethics of their behaviour and attitudes; adjudicating complaints of unethical behaviour; and, taking corrective action when warranted.

This Code articulates ethical principles, values, and standards to guide all members of the Canadian Psychological Association, whether scientists, practitioners, or scientist practitioners, or whether acting in a research, direct service, teaching, student, trainee, administrative, management, employer, employee, supervisory, consultative, peer review, editorial, expert witness, social policy, or any other role related to the discipline of psychology.

Structure and Derivation of Code

Structure. Four ethical principles, to be considered and balanced in ethical decision making, are presented. Each principle is followed by a statement of those values that are included in and give definition to the principle. Each values statement is followed by a list of ethical standards that illustrate the application of the specific principle and values to the activities of psychologists. The standards range from minimal behavioural expectations (e.g., Standards I.28, II.28, III.33, IV.27) to more idealized, but achievable, attitudinal and behavioural expectations (e.g., Standards I.12, II.12, III.10, IV.6). In the margin, to the left of the standards, key words are placed to guide the reader through the standards and to illustrate the relationship of the specific standards to the values statement.

Derivation. The four principles represent those ethical principles used most consistently by Canadian psychologists to resolve hypothetical ethical dilemmas sent to them by the CPA Committee on Ethics during the initial development of the Code. In addition to the responses provided by Canadian psychologists, the values statements and ethical standards have been derived from interdisciplinary and international ethics codes, provincial and specialty codes of conduct, and ethics literature.

WHEN PRINCIPLES CONFLICT

Principle I: Respect for the Dignity of Persons. This principle, with its emphasis on moral rights, generally should be given the highest weight, except in circumstances in which there is a clear and imminent danger to the physical safety of any person.

Principle II: Responsible Caring. This principle generally should be given the second highest weight. Responsible caring requires competence and should be carried out only in ways that respect the dignity of persons.

Principle III: Integrity in Relationships. This principle generally should be given the third highest weight. Psychologists are expected to demonstrate the highest integrity in all of their relationships. However, in rare circumstances, values such as openness and straightforwardness might need to be subordinated to the values contained in the Principles of Respect for the Dignity of Persons and Responsible Caring.

Principle IV: Responsibility to Society. This principle generally should be given the lowest weight of the four principles when it conflicts with one or more of them. Although it is necessary and important to consider responsibility to society in every ethical decision, adherence to this principle must be subject to and guided by Respect for the Dignity of Persons, Responsible Caring, and Integrity in Relationships. When a person's welfare appears to conflict with benefits to society, it is often possible to find ways of working for the benefit of society that do not violate respect and responsible caring for the person. However, if this is not possible, the dignity and well-being of a person should not be sacrificed to a vision of the greater good of society, and greater weight must be given to respect and responsible caring for the person.

Even with the above ordering of the principles, psychologists will be faced with ethical dilemmas that are difficult to resolve. In these circumstances, psychologists are expected to engage in an ethical decision-making process that is explicit enough to bear public scrutiny. In some cases, resolution might be a matter of personal conscience. However, decisions of personal conscience are also expected to be the result of a decision-making process that is based on a reasonably coherent set of ethical principles and that can bear public scrutiny. If the psychologist can demonstrate that every reasonable effort was made to apply the ethical principles of this Code and resolution of the conflict has had to depend on the personal conscience of the psychologist, such a psychologist would be deemed to have followed this Code.

THE ETHICAL DECISION-MAKING PROCESS

The ethical decision-making process might occur very rapidly, leading to an easy resolution of an ethical issue. This is particularly true of issues for which clear-cut guidelines or standards exist and for which there is no conflict between principles. On the other hand, some ethical issues (particularly those in which ethical principles conflict) are not easily resolved, might be emotionally distressful, and might require time-consuming deliberation.

The following basic steps typify approaches to ethical decision making:

1. Identification of the individuals and groups potentially affected by the decision.
2. Identification of ethically relevant issues and practices, including the interests, rights, and any relevant characteristics of the

individuals and groups involved and of the system or circumstances in which the ethical problem arose.

3. Consideration of how personal biases, stresses, or self-interest might influence the development of or choice between courses of action.

4. Development of alternative courses of action.

5. Analysis of likely short-term, ongoing, and long-term risks and benefits of each course of action on the individual(s)/group(s) involved or likely to be affected (e.g., client, client's family or employees, employing institution, students, research participants, colleagues, the discipline, society, self).

6. Choice of course of action after conscientious application of existing principles, values, and standards.

7. Action, with a commitment to assume responsibility for the consequences of the action.

8. Evaluation of the results of the course of action.

9. Assumption of responsibility for consequences of action, including correction of negative consequences, if any, or re-engaging in the decision-making process if the ethical issue is not resolved.

10. Appropriate action, as warranted and feasible, to prevent future occurrences of the dilemma (e.g., communication and problem solving with colleagues; changes in procedures and practices).

Psychologists engaged in time-consuming deliberation are encouraged and expected to consult with parties affected by the ethical problem, when appropriate, and with colleagues and/or advisory bodies when such persons can add knowledge or objectivity to the decision-making process. Although the decision for action remains with the individual psychologist, the seeking and consideration of such assistance reflects an ethical approach to ethical decision making.

USES OF THE CODE

This Code is intended to guide psychologists in their everyday conduct, thinking, and planning, and in the resolution of ethical dilemmas; that is, it advocates the practice of both proactive and reactive ethics.

The Code also is intended to serve as an umbrella document for the development of codes of conduct or other more specific codes. For example, the Code could be used as an ethical framework for the identification of behaviours that would be considered enforceable in a jurisdiction, the violation of which would constitute misconduct; or, jurisdictions could identify those standards in the Code that would be considered of a more serious nature and, therefore, reportable and subject to possible discipline. In addition, the principles and values could be used to help specialty areas develop standards that are specific to those areas. Some work in this direction has already occurred within CPA (e.g., Guidelines for the Use of Animals in Research and Instruction in Psychology, Guidelines for Non-Discriminatory Practice, Guidelines for Psychologists in Addressing Recovered Memories). The principles and values incorporated into this Code, insofar as they come to be reflected in other documents guiding the behaviour of psychologists, will reduce inconsistency and conflict between documents.

A third use of the Code is to assist in the adjudication of complaints against psychologists. A body charged with this responsibility is required to investigate allegations, judge whether unacceptable behaviour has occurred, and determine what corrective action should be taken. In judging whether unacceptable conduct has occurred, many jurisdictions refer to a code of conduct. Some complaints, however, are about conduct that is not addressed directly in a code of conduct. The Code provides an ethical framework for determining whether the complaint is of enough concern, either at the level of the individual psychologist or at the level of the profession as a whole, to warrant corrective action (e.g., discipline of the individual psychologist, general educational activities for members, or incorporation into the code of conduct). In determining corrective action for an individual psychologist, one of the judgments the adjudicating body needs to make is whether an individual conscientiously engaged in an ethical decision-making process and acted in good faith, or whether there was a negligent or willful disregard of ethical principles. The articulation of the ethical decision-making process contained in this Code provides guidance for making such judgments.

RESPONSIBILITY OF THE INDIVIDUAL PSYCHOLOGIST

The discipline's contract with society commits the discipline and its members to act as a moral community that develops its ethical awareness and sensitivity, educates new members in the ethics of the discipline, manages its affairs and its members in an ethical manner, is as self-correcting as possible, and is accountable both internally and externally.

However, responsibility for ethical action depends foremost on the integrity of each individual psychologist; that is, on each psychologist's commitment to behave as ethically as possible in every situation.

Acceptance to membership in the Canadian Psychological Association, a scientific and professional association of psychologists, commits members:

1. To adhere to the Association's Code in all current activities as a psychologist.
2. To apply conscientiously the ethical principles and values of the Code to new and emerging areas of activity.
3. To assess and discuss ethical issues and practices with colleagues on a regular basis.
4. To bring to the attention of the Association ethical issues that require clarification or the development of new guidelines or standards.
5. To bring concerns about possible unethical actions by a psychologist directly to the psychologist when the action appears to be primarily a lack of sensitivity, knowledge, or experience, and attempt to reach an agreement on the issue and, if needed, on the appropriate action to be taken.
6. To bring concerns about possible unethical actions of a more serious nature (e.g., actions that have caused or could cause serious harm, or actions that are considered misconduct in the jurisdiction) to the person(s) or body(ies) best suited to investigating the situation and to stopping or offsetting the harm.
7. To consider seriously others' concerns about one's own possibly unethical actions and attempt to reach an agreement on the issue and, if needed, take appropriate action.
8. In bringing or in responding to concerns about possible unethical actions, not to be vexatious or malicious.
9. To cooperate with duly constituted committees of the Association that are concerned with ethics and ethical conduct.

RELATIONSHIP OF CODE TO PERSONAL BEHAVIOUR

This Code is intended to guide and regulate only those activities a psychologist engages in by virtue of being a psychologist. There is no intention to guide or regulate a psychologist's activities outside of this context. Personal behaviour becomes a concern of the discipline only if it is of such a nature that it undermines public trust in the discipline as a whole or if it raises questions about the psychologist's ability to carry out appropriately his/her responsibilities as a psychologist.

RELATIONSHIP OF CODE TO PROVINCIAL REGULATORY BODIES

In exercising its responsibility to articulate ethical principles, values, and standards for those who wish to become and remain members in good standing, the Canadian Psychological Association recognizes the multiple memberships that some psychologists have (both regulatory and voluntary). The Code has attempted to encompass and incorporate those ethical principles most prevalent in the discipline as a whole, thereby minimizing the possibility of variance with provincial/territorial regulations and guidelines. Psychologists are expected to respect the requirements of their provincial/territorial regulatory bodies. Such requirements might define particular behaviours that constitute misconduct, are reportable to the regulatory body, and/or are subject to discipline.

DEFINITION OF TERMS

For the purposes of this Code:

a. "Psychologist" means any person who is a Fellow, Member, Student Affiliate or Foreign Affiliate of the Canadian Psychological Association, or a member of any psychology voluntary association or regulatory body adopting this Code. (Readers are reminded that provincial/territorial jurisdictions might restrict the legal use of the term psychologist in their jurisdiction and that such restrictions are to be honoured.)

b. "Client" means an individual, family, or group (including an organization or community) receiving service from a psychologist.

c. Clients, research participants, students, and any other persons with whom psychologists come in contact in the course of their work, are "independent" if they can independently contract or give informed consent. Such persons are "partially dependent" if the decision to contract or give informed consent is shared between two or more parties (e.g., parents and school boards, workers and Workers' Compensation Boards, adult members of a family). Such persons are considered to be "fully dependent" if they have little or no choice about whether or not to receive service or participate in an activity (e.g., patients who have been involuntarily committed to a psychiatric facility, or very young children involved in a research project).

d. "Others" means any persons with whom psychologists come in contact in the course of their work. This may include, but is not limited to: clients seeking help with individual, family, organizational, industrial, or community issues; research participants; employees; students; trainees; supervisees; colleagues; employers; third party payers; and, members of the general public.

e. "Legal or civil rights" means those rights protected under laws and statutes recognized by the province or territory in which the psychologist is working.

f. "Moral rights" means fundamental and inalienable human rights that might or might not be fully protected by existing laws and statutes. Of particular significance to psychologists, for example, are rights to: distributive justice; fairness and due process; and, developmentally appropriate privacy, self-determination, and personal liberty. Protection of some aspects of these rights might involve practices that are not contained or controlled within current laws and statutes. Moral rights are not limited to those mentioned in this definition.

g. "Unjust discrimination" or "unjustly discriminatory" means activities that are prejudicial or promote prejudice to persons because of their culture, nationality, ethnicity, colour, race, religion, sex, gender, marital status, sexual orientation, physical or mental abilities, age, socio-economic status, or any other preference or personal characteristic, condition, or status.

h. "Sexual harassment" includes either or both of the following:
(i) The use of power or authority in an attempt to coerce another person to engage in or tolerate sexual activity. Such uses include explicit or implicit threats of reprisal for noncompliance, or promises of reward for compliance.
(ii) Engaging in deliberate and/or repeated unsolicited sexually oriented comments, anecdotes, gestures, or touching, if such behaviours: are offensive and unwelcome; create an offensive, hostile, or intimidating working, learning, or service environment; or, can be expected to be harmful to the recipient.[3]

i. The "discipline of psychology" refers to the scientific and applied methods and knowledge of psychology, and to the structures and procedures used by its members for conducting their work in relationship to society, to members of the public, to students or trainees, and to each other.

REVIEW SCHEDULE

To maintain the relevance and responsiveness of this Code, it will be reviewed regularly by the CPA Board of Directors, and revised as needed. You are invited to forward comments and suggestions, at any time, to the CPA office. In addition to psychologists, this invitation is extended to all readers, including members of the public and other disciplines.

PRINCIPLE I:
RESPECT FOR THE DIGNITY OF PERSONS

Values Statement

In the course of their work as scientists, practitioners, or scientist-practitioners, psychologists come into contact with many different individuals and groups, including: research participants; clients seeking help with individual, family, organizational, industrial, or community issues; students; trainees; supervisees; employees; business partners; business competitors; colleagues; employers; third party payers; and, the general public.

In these contacts, psychologists accept as fundamental the principle of respect for the dignity of persons; that is, the belief that each person should be treated primarily as a person or an end in him/herself, not as an object or a means to an end. In so doing, psychologists acknowledge that all persons have a right to have their innate worth as human beings appreciated and that this worth is not dependent upon their culture, nationality, ethnicity, colour, race, religion, sex, gender, marital status, sexual orientation, physical or mental abilities, age, socio-economic status, or any other preference or personal characteristic, condition, or status.

Although psychologists have a responsibility to respect the dignity of all persons with whom they come in contact in their role as psychologists, the nature of their contract with society demands that their greatest responsibility be to those persons in the most vulnerable position. Normally, persons directly receiving or involved in the psychologist's activities are in such a position (e.g., research participants, clients, students). This responsibility is almost always greater than their responsibility to those indirectly involved (e.g., employers, third party payers, the general public).

Adherence to the concept of moral rights is an essential component of respect for the dignity of persons. Rights to privacy, self-determination, personal liberty, and natural justice are of particular importance to psychologists, and they have a responsibility to protect and promote these rights in all of their activities. As such, psychologists have a responsibility to develop and follow procedures for informed consent, confidentiality, fair treatment, and due process that are consistent with those rights.

As individual rights exist within the context of the rights of others and of responsible caring (see Principle II), there might be circumstances in which the possibility of serious detrimental consequences to themselves or others, a diminished capacity to be autonomous, or a court order, would disallow some aspects of the rights to privacy, self-determination, and personal liberty. Indeed, such circumstances might be serious enough to create a duty to warn or protect others (see Standards I.45 and II.39). However, psychologists still have a responsibility to respect the rights of the person(s) involved to the greatest extent possible under the circumstances, and to do what is necessary and reasonable to reduce the need for future disallowances.

Psychologists recognize that, although all persons possess moral rights, the manner in which such rights are promoted, protected, and exercised varies across communities and cultures. For instance, definitions of what is considered private vary, as does the role of families and other community members in personal decision making. In their work, psychologists acknowledge and respect such differences, while guarding against clear violations of moral rights.

In addition, psychologists recognize that as individual, family, group, or community vulnerabilities increase, or as the power of persons to control their environment or their lives decreases, psychologists have an increasing responsibility to seek ethical advice and to establish safeguards to protect the rights of the persons involved. For this reason, psychologists consider it their responsibility to increase safeguards to protect and promote the rights of persons involved in their activities proportionate to the degree of dependency and the lack of voluntary initiation. For example, this would mean that there would be more safeguards to protect and promote the rights of fully dependent persons than partially dependent persons, and more safeguards for partially dependent than independent persons.

Respect for the dignity of persons also includes the concept of distributive justice. With respect to psychologists, this concept implies that all persons are entitled to benefit equally from the contributions of psychology and to equal quality in the processes, procedures, and services being conducted by psychologists, regardless of the person's characteristics, condition, or status. Although individual psychologists might specialize and direct their activities to particular populations, or might decline to engage in activities based on the limits of their competence or acknowledgment of problems in some relationships, psychologists must not exclude persons on a capricious or unjustly discriminatory basis.

By virtue of the social contract that the discipline has with society, psychologists have a higher duty of care to members of society than the general duty of care all members of society have to each other. However, psychologists are entitled to protect themselves from serious violations of their own moral rights (e.g., privacy, personal liberty) in carrying out their work as psychologists.

Ethical Standards

In adhering to the Principle of Respect for the Dignity of Persons, psychologists would:

General respect

I.1 Demonstrate appropriate respect for the knowledge, insight, experience, and areas of expertise of others.

I.2 Not engage publicly (e.g., in public statements, presentations, research reports, or with clients) in degrading comments about others, including demeaning jokes based on such characteristics as culture, nationality, ethnicity, colour, race, religion, sex, gender, or sexual orientation.

I.3 Strive to use language that conveys respect for the dignity of persons as much as possible in all written or oral communication.

I.4 Abstain from all forms of harassment, including sexual harassment.

General rights

I.5 Avoid or refuse to participate in practices disrespectful of the legal, civil, or moral rights of others.

I.6 Refuse to advise, train, or supply information to anyone who, in the psychologist's judgment, will use the knowledge or skills to infringe on human rights.

I.7 Make every reasonable effort to ensure that psychological knowledge is not misused, intentionally or unintentionally, to infringe on human rights.

I.8 Respect the right of research participants, clients, employees, supervisees, students, trainees, and others to safeguard their own dignity.

Non-discrimination

I.9 Not practice, condone, facilitate, or collaborate with any form of unjust discrimination.

I.10 Act to correct practices that are unjustly discriminatory.

1.11   Seek to design research, teaching, practice, and business activities in such a way that they contribute to the fair distribution of benefits to individuals and groups, and that they do not unfairly exclude those who are vulnerable or might be disadvantaged.

Fair treatment/due process

1.12   Work and act in a spirit of fair treatment to others.

1.13   Help to establish and abide by due process or other natural justice procedures for employment, evaluation, adjudication, editorial, and peer review activities.

1.14   Compensate others fairly for the use of their time, energy, and knowledge, unless such compensation is refused in advance.

1.15   Establish fees that are fair in light of the time, energy, and knowledge of the psychologist and any associates or employees, and in light of the market value of the product or service. (Also see Standard IV.12.)

Informed consent

1.16   Seek as full and active participation as possible from others in decisions that affect them, respecting and integrating as much as possible their opinions and wishes.

1.17   Recognize that informed consent is the result of a process of reaching an agreement to work collaboratively, rather than of simply having a consent form signed.

1.18   Respect the expressed wishes of persons to involve others (e.g., family members, community members) in their decision making regarding informed consent. This would include respect for written and clearly expressed unwritten advance directives.

1.19   Obtain informed consent from all independent and partially dependent persons for any psychological services provided to them except in circumstances of urgent need (e.g., disaster or other crisis). In urgent circumstances, psychologists would proceed with the assent of such persons, but fully informed consent would be obtained as soon as possible. (Also see Standard 1.29.)

1.20   Obtain informed consent for all research activities that involve obtrusive measures, invasion of privacy, more than minimal risk of harm, or any attempt to change the behaviour of research participants.

I.21   Establish and use signed consent forms that specify the
        dimensions of informed consent or that acknowledge that
        such dimensions have been explained and are understood, if
        such forms are required by law or if such forms are desired
        by the psychologist, the person(s) giving consent, or the
        organization for whom the psychologist works.

I.22   Accept and document oral consent, in situations in which
        signed consent forms are not acceptable culturally or in
        which there are other good reasons for not using them.

I.23   Provide, in obtaining informed consent, as much information
        as reasonable or prudent persons would want to know before
        making a decision or consenting to the activity. The
        psychologist would relay this information in language that
        the persons understand (including providing translation into
        another language, if necessary) and would take whatever
        reasonable steps are needed to ensure that the information
        was, in fact, understood.

I.24   Ensure, in the process of obtaining informed consent, that at
        least the following points are understood: purpose and nature
        of the activity; mutual responsibilities; confidentiality
        protections and limitations; likely benefits and risks;
        alternatives; the likely consequences of non-action; the option
        to refuse or withdraw at any time, without prejudice; over
        what period of time the consent applies; and, how to rescind
        consent if desired. (Also see Standards III.23–30.)

I.25   Provide new information in a timely manner, whenever such
        information becomes available and is significant enough that
        it reasonably could be seen as relevant to the original or
        ongoing informed consent.

I.26   Clarify the nature of multiple relationships to all concerned
        parties before obtaining consent, if providing services to or
        conducting research at the request or for the use of third
        parties. This would include, but not be limited to: the
        purpose of the service or research; the reasonably anticipated
        use that will be made of information collected; and, the limits
        on confidentiality. Third parties may include schools, courts,
        government agencies, insurance companies, police, and
        special funding bodies.

Freedom of consent

1.27   Take all reasonable steps to ensure that consent is not given under conditions of coercion, undue pressure, or undue reward. (Also see Standard III.32.)

1.28   Not proceed with any research activity, if consent is given under any condition of coercion, undue pressure, or undue reward. (Also see Standard III.32.)

1.29   Take all reasonable steps to confirm or re-establish freedom of consent, if consent for service is given under conditions of duress or conditions of extreme need.

1.30   Respect the right of persons to discontinue participation or service at any time, and be responsive to non-verbal indications of a desire to discontinue if a person has difficulty with verbally communicating such a desire (e.g., young children, verbally disabled persons) or, due to culture, is unlikely to communicate such a desire orally.

Protections for vulnerable persons

1.31   Seek an independent and adequate ethical review of human rights issues and protections for any research involving members of vulnerable groups, including persons of diminished capacity to give informed consent, before making a decision to proceed.

1.32   Not use persons of diminished capacity to give informed consent in research studies, if the research involved may be carried out equally well with persons who have a fuller capacity to give informed consent.

1.33   Seek to use methods that maximize the understanding and ability to consent of persons of diminished capacity to give informed consent, and that reduce the need for a substitute decision maker.

1.34   Carry out informed consent processes with those persons who are legally responsible or appointed to give informed consent on behalf of persons not competent to consent on their own behalf, seeking to ensure respect for any previously expressed preferences of persons not competent to consent.

1.35   Seek willing and adequately informed participation from any person of diminished capacity to give informed consent, and proceed without this assent only if the service or research activity is considered to be of direct benefit to that person.

1.36   Be particularly cautious in establishing the freedom of consent of any person who is in a dependent relationship to the psychologist (e.g., student, employee). This may include,

but is not limited to, offering that person an alternative
activity to fulfill their educational or employment goals,
or offering a range of research studies or experience
opportunities from which the person can select, none
of which is so onerous as to be coercive.

Privacy

1.37 Seek and collect only information that is germane to the
purpose(s) for which consent has been obtained.

1.38 Take care not to infringe, in research, teaching, or service
activities, on the personally, developmentally, or culturally
defined private space of individuals or groups, unless clear
permission is granted to do so.

1.39 Record only that private information necessary for the
provision of continuous, coordinated service, or for the goals
of the particular research study being conducted, or that is
required or justified by law. (Also see Standards IV.17 and
IV.18.)

1.40 Respect the right of research participants, employees,
supervisees, students, and trainees to reasonable personal
privacy.

1.41 Collect, store, handle, and transfer all private information,
whether written or unwritten (e.g., communication during
service provision, written records, e-mail or fax communication,
computer files, video-tapes), in a way that attends to the
needs for privacy and security. This would include having
adequate plans for records in circumstances of one's own
serious illness, termination of employment, or death.

1.42 Take all reasonable steps to ensure that records over which
they have control remain personally identifiable only as long
as necessary in the interests of those to whom they refer and/or
to the research project for which they were collected, or as
required or justified by law (e.g., the possible need to defend
oneself against future allegations), and render anonymous or
destroy any records under their control that no longer need to
be personally identifiable. (Also see Standards IV.17 and IV.18.)

Confidentiality

1.43 Be careful not to relay information about colleagues, colleagues'
clients, research participants, employees, supervisees, students,
trainees, and members of organizations, gained in the process
of their activities as psychologists, that the psychologist

has reason to believe is considered confidential by those persons, except as required or justified by law. (Also see Standards IV.17 and IV.18.)

1.44 Clarify what measures will be taken to protect confidentiality, and what responsibilities family, group, and community members have for the protection of each other's confidentiality, when engaged in services to or research with individuals, families, groups, or communities.

1.45 Share confidential information with others only with the informed consent of those involved, or in a manner that the persons involved cannot be identified, except as required or justified by law, or in circumstances of actual or possible serious physical harm or death. (Also see Standards II.39, IV.17, and IV.18.)

Extended responsibility

1.46 Encourage others, in a manner consistent with this Code, to respect the dignity of persons and to expect respect for their own dignity.

1.47 Assume overall responsibility for the scientific and professional activities of their assistants, employees, students, supervisees, and trainees with regard to Respect for the Dignity of Persons, all of whom, however, incur similar obligations.

PRINCIPLE II:
RESPONSIBLE CARING

Values Statement

A basic ethical expectation of any discipline is that its activities will benefit members of society or, at least, do no harm. Therefore, psychologists demonstrate an active concern for the welfare of any individual, family, group, or community with whom they relate in their role as psychologists. This concern includes both those directly involved and those indirectly involved in their activities. However, as with Principle I, psychologists' greatest responsibility is to protect the welfare of those in the most vulnerable position. Normally, persons directly involved in their activities (e.g., research participants, clients, students) are in such a position. Psychologists' responsibility to those indirectly involved (e.g., employers, third party payers, the general public) normally is secondary.

As persons usually consider their own welfare in their personal decision making, obtaining informed consent (see Principle 1) is one of the best methods for ensuring that their welfare will be protected. However, it is only when such consent is combined with the responsible caring of the psychologist that there is considerable ethical protection of the welfare of the person(s) involved.

Responsible caring leads psychologists to take care to discern the potential harm and benefits involved, to predict the likelihood of their occurrence, to proceed only if the potential benefits outweigh the potential harms, to develop and use methods that will minimize harms and maximize benefits, and to take responsibility for correcting clearly harmful effects that have occurred as a direct result of their research, teaching, practice, or business activities.

In order to carry out these steps, psychologists recognize the need for competence and self-knowledge. They consider incompetent action to be unethical per se, as it is unlikely to be of benefit and likely to be harmful. They engage only in those activities in which they have competence or for which they are receiving supervision, and they perform their activities as competently as possible. They acquire, contribute to, and use the existing knowledge most relevant to the best interests of those concerned. They also engage in self-reflection regarding how their own values, attitudes, experiences, and social context (e.g., culture, ethnicity, colour, religion, sex, gender, sexual orientation, physical and mental abilities, age, and socio-economic status) influence their actions, interpretations, choices, and recommendations. This is done with the intent of increasing the probability that their activities will benefit and not harm the individuals, families, groups, and communities to whom they relate in their role as psychologists. Psychologists define harm and benefit in terms of both physical and psychological dimensions. They are concerned about such factors as: social, family, and community relationships; personal and cultural identity; feelings of self-worth, fear, humiliation, interpersonal trust, and cynicism; self-knowledge and general knowledge; and, such factors as physical safety, comfort, pain, and injury. They are concerned about immediate, short-term, and long-term effects.

Responsible caring recognizes and respects (e.g., through obtaining informed consent) the ability of individuals, families, groups, and communities to make decisions for themselves and to care for themselves and each other. It does not replace or undermine such ability, nor does it substitute one person's opinion about what is in the best interests of another person for that other person's competent decision making. However, psychologists recognize that, as vulnerabilities increase or as power to control one's own life decreases, psychologists have an increasing responsibility to protect the well-being of the individual, family, group, or community involved. For this reason, as in Principle I, psychologists consider it their responsibility to increase safeguards proportionate to the degree of dependency and the lack of voluntary initiation on the part of the persons involved. However, for Principle II, the safeguards are for the well-being of persons rather than for the rights of persons.

Psychologists' treatment and use of animals in their research and teaching activities are also a component of responsible caring. Although animals do not have the same moral rights as persons (e.g., privacy), they do have the right to be treated humanely and not to be exposed to unnecessary discomfort, pain, or disruption.

By virtue of the social contract that the discipline has with society, psychologists have a higher duty of care to members of society than the general duty of care all members of society have to each other. However, psychologists are entitled to protect their own basic well-being (e.g., physical safety, family relationships) in their work as psychologists.

Ethical Standards
In adhering to the Principle of Responsible Caring, psychologists would:

General caring
II.1 Protect and promote the welfare of clients, research participants, employees, supervisees, students, trainees, colleagues, and others.

II.2 Avoid doing harm to clients, research participants, employees, supervisees, students, trainees, colleagues, and others.

II.3 Accept responsibility for the consequences of their actions.

II.4 Refuse to advise, train, or supply information to anyone who, in the psychologist's judgment, will use the knowledge or skills to harm others.

II.5 Make every reasonable effort to ensure that psychological knowledge is not misused, intentionally or unintentionally, to harm others.

Competence and self-knowledge
II.6 Offer or carry out (without supervision) only those activities for which they have established their competence to carry them out to the benefit of others.

II.7 Not delegate activities to persons not competent to carry them out to the benefit of others.

II.8 Take immediate steps to obtain consultation or to refer a client to a colleague or other appropriate professional, whichever is more likely to result in providing the client with competent service, if it becomes apparent that a client's problems are beyond their competence.

II.9 Keep themselves up to date with a broad range of relevant knowledge, research methods, and techniques, and their impact on persons and society, through the reading of relevant literature, peer consultation, and continuing education activities, in order that their service or research activities and conclusions will benefit and not harm others.

II.10 Evaluate how their own experiences, attitudes, culture, beliefs, values, social context, individual differences, specific training, and stresses influence their interactions with others, and integrate this awareness into all efforts to benefit and not harm others.

II.11 Seek appropriate help and/or discontinue scientific or professional activity for an appropriate period of time, if a physical or psychological condition reduces their ability to benefit and not harm others.

II.12 Engage in self-care activities that help to avoid conditions (e.g., burnout, addictions) that could result in impaired judgment and interfere with their ability to benefit and not harm others.

Risk/benefit analysis

II.13 Assess the individuals, families, groups, and communities involved in their activities adequately enough to ensure that they will be able to discern what will benefit and not harm the persons involved.

II.14 Be sufficiently sensitive to and knowledgeable about individual, group, community, and cultural differences and vulnerabilities to discern what will benefit and not harm persons involved in their activities.

II.15 Carry out pilot studies to determine the effects of all new procedures and techniques that might carry more than minimal risk, before considering their use on a broader scale.

II.16 Seek an independent and adequate ethical review of the balance of risks and potential benefits of all research and new interventions that involve procedures of unknown consequence, or where pain, discomfort, or harm are possible, before making a decision to proceed.

II.17 Not carry out any scientific or professional activity unless the probable benefit is proportionately greater than the risk involved.

Maximize benefit

II.18 Provide services that are coordinated over time and with other service providers, in order to avoid duplication or working at cross purposes.

II.19 Create and maintain records relating to their activities that are sufficient to support continuity and appropriate coordination of their activities with the activities of others.

II.20 Make themselves aware of the knowledge and skills of other disciplines (e.g., law, medicine, business administration) and advise the use of such knowledge and skills, where relevant to the benefit of others.

II.21 Strive to provide and/or obtain the best possible service for those needing and seeking psychological service. This may include, but is not limited to: selecting interventions that are relevant to the needs and characteristics of the client and that have reasonable theoretical or empirically-supported efficacy in light of those needs and characteristics; consulting with, or including in service delivery, persons relevant to the culture or belief systems of those served; advocating on behalf of the client; and, recommending professionals other than psychologists when appropriate.

II.22 Monitor and evaluate the effect of their activities, record their findings, and communicate new knowledge to relevant others.

II.23 Debrief research participants in such a way that the participants' knowledge is enhanced and the participants have a sense of contribution to knowledge. (Also see Standards III.26 and III.27.)

II.24 Perform their teaching duties on the basis of careful preparation, so that their instruction is current and scholarly.

II.25 Facilitate the professional and scientific development of their employees, supervisees, students, and trainees by ensuring that these persons understand the values and ethical prescriptions of the discipline, and by providing or arranging for adequate working conditions, timely evaluations, and constructive consultation and experience opportunities.

II.26 Encourage and assist students in publication of worthy student papers.

Minimize harm

II.27 Be acutely aware of the power relationship in therapy and, therefore, not encourage or engage in sexual intimacy with therapy clients, neither during therapy, nor for that period of time following therapy during which the power relationship reasonably could be expected to influence the client's personal decision making. (Also see Standard III.31.)

II.28 Not encourage or engage in sexual intimacy with students or trainees with whom the psychologist has an evaluative or other relationship of direct authority. (Also see Standard III.31.)

II.29 Be careful not to engage in activities in a way that could place incidentally involved persons at risk.

II.30 Be acutely aware of the need for discretion in the recording and communication of information, in order that the information not be misinterpreted or misused to the detriment of others. This includes, but is not limited to: not recording information that could lead to misinterpretation and misuse; avoiding conjecture; clearly labelling opinion; and, communicating information in language that can be understood clearly by the recipient of the information.

II.31 Give reasonable assistance to secure needed psychological services or activities, if personally unable to meet requests for needed psychological services or activities.

II.32 Provide a client, if appropriate and if desired by the client, with reasonable assistance to find a way to receive needed services in the event that third party payments are exhausted and the client cannot afford the fees involved.

II.33 Maintain appropriate contact, support, and responsibility for caring until a colleague or other professional begins service, if referring a client to a colleague or other professional.

II.34 Give reasonable notice and be reasonably assured that discontinuation will cause no harm to the client, before discontinuing services.

II.35 Screen appropriate research participants and select those least likely to be harmed, if more than minimal risk of harm to some research participants is possible.

II.36 Act to minimize the impact of their research activities on research participants' personalities, or on their physical or mental integrity.

Offset/correct harm

11.37 Terminate an activity when it is clear that the activity carries more than minimal risk of harm and is found to be more harmful than beneficial, or when the activity is no longer needed.

11.38 Refuse to help individuals, families, groups, or communities to carry out or submit to activities that, according to current knowledge, or legal or professional guidelines, would cause serious physical or psychological harm to themselves or others.

11.39 Do everything reasonably possible to stop or offset the consequences of actions by others when these actions are likely to cause serious physical harm or death. This may include reporting to appropriate authorities (e.g., the police), an intended victim, or a family member or other support person who can intervene, and would be done even when a confidential relationship is involved. (Also see Standard 1.45.)

11.40 Act to stop or offset the consequences of seriously harmful activities being carried out by another psychologist or member of another discipline, when there is objective information about the activities and the harm, and when these activities have come to their attention outside of a confidential client relationship between themselves and the psychologist or member of another discipline. This may include reporting to the appropriate regulatory body, authority, or committee for action, depending on the psychologist's judgment about the person(s) or body(ies) best suited to stop or offset the harm, and depending upon regulatory requirements and definitions of misconduct.

11.41 Act also to stop or offset the consequences of harmful activities carried out by another psychologist or member of another discipline, when the harm is not serious or the activities appear to be primarily a lack of sensitivity, knowledge, or experience, and when the activities have come to their attention outside of a confidential client relationship between themselves and the psychologist or member of another discipline. This may include talking informally with the psychologist or member of the other discipline, obtaining objective information and, if possible and relevant, the assurance that the harm will discontinue and be corrected. If in a vulnerable position (e.g., employee, trainee) with respect to the other psychologist or member of the other discipline, it may include asking persons in less vulnerable positions to participate in the meeting(s).

II.42 Be open to the concerns of others about perceptions of harm that they as a psychologist might be causing, stop activities that are causing harm, and not punish or seek punishment for those who raise such concerns in good faith.

II.43 Not place an individual, group, family, or community needing service at a serious disadvantage by offering them no service in order to fulfill the conditions of a research design, when a standard service is available.

II.44 Debrief research participants in such a way that any harm caused can be discerned, and act to correct any resultant harm. (Also see Standards III.26 and III.27.)

Care of animals

II.45 Not use animals in their research unless there is a reasonable expectation that the research will increase understanding of the structures and processes underlying behaviour, or increase understanding of the particular animal species used in the study, or result eventually in benefits to the health and welfare of humans or other animals.

II.46 Use a procedure subjecting animals to pain, stress, or privation only if an alternative procedure is unavailable and the goal is justified by its prospective scientific, educational, or applied value.

II.47 Make every effort to minimize the discomfort, illness, and pain of animals. This would include performing surgical procedures only under appropriate anaesthesia, using techniques to avoid infection and minimize pain during and after surgery and, if disposing of experimental animals is carried out at the termination of the study, doing so in a humane way.

II.48 Use animals in classroom demonstrations only if the instructional objectives cannot be achieved through the use of video-tapes, films, or other methods, and if the type of demonstration is warranted by the anticipated instructional gain.

Extended responsibility

II.49 Encourage others, in a manner consistent with this Code, to care responsibly.

II.50 Assume overall responsibility for the scientific and professional activities of their assistants, employees, supervisees, students, and trainees with regard to the Principle of Responsible Caring, all of whom, however, incur similar obligations.

PRINCIPLE III:
INTEGRITY IN RELATIONSHIPS

Values Statement

The relationships formed by psychologists in the course of their work embody explicit and implicit mutual expectations of integrity that are vital to the advancement of scientific knowledge and to the maintenance of public confidence in the discipline of psychology. These expectations include: accuracy and honesty; straightforwardness and openness; the maximization of objectivity and minimization of bias; and, avoidance of conflicts of interest. Psychologists have a responsibility to meet these expectations and to encourage reciprocity.

In addition to accuracy, honesty, and the obvious prohibitions of fraud or misrepresentation, meeting expectations of integrity is enhanced by self-knowledge and the use of critical analysis. Although it can be argued that science is value-free and impartial, scientists are not. Personal values and self-interest can affect the questions psychologists ask, how they ask those questions, what assumptions they make, their selection of methods, what they observe and what they fail to observe, and how they interpret their data.

Psychologists are not expected to be value-free or totally without self-interest in conducting their activities. However, they are expected to understand how their backgrounds, personal needs, and values interact with their activities, to be open and honest about the influence of such factors, and to be as objective and unbiased as possible under the circumstances.

The values of openness and straightforwardness exist within the context of Respect for the Dignity of Persons (Principle I) and Responsible Caring (Principle II). As such, there will be circumstances in which openness and straightforwardness will need to be tempered. Fully open and straightforward disclosure might not be needed or desired by others and, in some circumstances, might be a risk to their dignity or well-being, or considered culturally inappropriate. In such circumstances, however, psychologists have a responsibility to ensure that their decision not to be fully open or straightforward is justified by higher-order values and does not invalidate any informed consent procedures.

Of special concern to psychologists is the provision of incomplete disclosure when obtaining informed consent for research participation, or temporarily leading research participants to believe that a research project has a purpose other than its actual purpose. These actions sometimes occur in research where full disclosure would be likely to influence the responses of the research participants and thus invalidate the results. Although research that uses such techniques can lead to knowledge that is beneficial, such benefits must be weighed against the research participant's right to self-determination and the importance of public and individual trust in psychology. Psychologists have a serious obligation to avoid as much as possible the use of such research procedures. They also have a serious obligation to consider the need for, the possible consequences of, and their responsibility to correct any resulting mistrust or other harmful effects from their use.

As public trust in the discipline of psychology includes trusting that psychologists will act in the best interests of members of the public, situations that present real or potential conflicts of interest are of concern to psychologists. Conflict-of-interest situations are those that can lead to distorted judgment and can motivate psychologists to act in ways that meet their own personal, political, financial, or business interests at the expense of the best interests of members of the public. Although avoidance of all conflicts of interest and potential exploitation of others is not possible, some are of such a high risk to protecting the interests of members of the public and to maintaining the trust of the public, that they are considered never acceptable (see Standard III.31). The risk level of other conflicts of interest (e.g., dual or multiple relationships) might be partially dependent on cultural factors and the specific type of professional relationship (e.g., long-term psychotherapy vs. community development activities). It is the responsibility of psychologists to avoid dual or multiple relationships and other conflicts of interest when appropriate and possible. When such situations cannot be avoided or are inappropriate to avoid, psychologists have a responsibility to declare that they have a conflict of interest, to seek advice, and to establish safeguards to ensure that the best interests of members of the public are protected.

Integrity in relationships implies that psychologists, as a matter of honesty, have a responsibility to maintain competence in any specialty area for which they declare competence, whether or not they are currently practising in that area. It also requires that psychologists, in as much as they present themselves as members and representatives of a specific discipline, have a responsibility to actively rely on and be guided by that discipline and its guidelines and requirements.

Ethical Standards
In adhering to the Principle of Integrity in Relationships, psychologists would:

Accuracy/honesty

III.1   Not knowingly participate in, condone, or be associated with dishonesty, fraud, or misrepresentation.

III.2 Accurately represent their own and their colleagues' credentials, qualifications, education, experience, competence, and affiliations, in all spoken, written, or printed communications, being careful not to use descriptions or information that could be misinterpreted (e.g., citing membership in a voluntary association of psychologists as a testament of competence).

III.3 Carefully protect their own and their colleagues' credentials from being misrepresented by others, and act quickly to correct any such misrepresentation.

III.4 Maintain competence in their declared area(s) of psychological competence, as well as in their current area(s) of activity. (Also see Standard II.9.)

III.5 Accurately represent their own and their colleagues' activities, functions, contributions, and likely or actual outcomes of their activities (including research results) in all spoken, written, or printed communication. This includes, but is not limited to: advertisements of services or products; course and workshop descriptions; academic grading requirements; and, research reports.

III.6 Ensure that their own and their colleagues' activities, functions, contributions, and likely or actual outcomes of their activities (including research results) are not misrepresented by others, and act quickly to correct any such misrepresentation.

III.7 Take credit only for the work and ideas that they have actually done or generated, and give credit for work done or ideas contributed by others (including students), in proportion to their contribution.

III.8 Acknowledge the limitations of their own and their colleagues' knowledge, methods, findings, interventions, and views.

III.9. Not suppress disconfirming evidence of their own and their colleagues' findings and views, acknowledging alternative hypotheses and explanations.

Objectivity/lack of bias

III.10 Evaluate how their personal experiences, attitudes, values, social context, individual differences, stresses, and specific training influence their activities and thinking, integrating this awareness into all attempts to be objective and unbiased in their research, service, and other activities.

III.11 Take care to communicate as completely and objectively as possible, and to clearly differentiate facts, opinions, theories, hypotheses, and ideas, when communicating knowledge, findings, and views.

III.12   Present instructional information accurately, avoiding bias in the selection and presentation of information, and publicly acknowledge any personal values or bias that influence the selection and presentation of information.

III.13   Act quickly to clarify any distortion by a sponsor, client, agency (e.g., news media), or other persons, of the findings of their research.

Straightforwardness/openness

III.14   Be clear and straightforward about all information needed to establish informed consent or any other valid written or unwritten agreement (for example: fees, including any limitations imposed by third-party payers; relevant business policies and practices; mutual concerns; mutual responsibilities; ethical responsibilities of psychologists; purpose and nature of the relationship, including research participation; alternatives; likely experiences; possible conflicts; possible outcomes; and, expectations for processing, using, and sharing any information generated).

III.15   Provide suitable information about the results of assessments, evaluations, or research findings to the persons involved, if appropriate and if asked. This information would be communicated in understandable language.

III.16   Fully explain reasons for their actions to persons who have been affected by their actions, if appropriate and if asked.

III.17   Honour all promises and commitments included in any written or verbal agreement, unless serious and unexpected circumstances (e.g., illness) intervene. If such circumstances occur, then the psychologist would make a full and honest explanation to other parties involved.

III.18   Make clear whether they are acting as private citizens, as members of specific organizations or groups, or as representatives of the discipline of psychology, when making statements or when involved in public activities.

III.19   Carry out, present, and discuss research in a way that is consistent with a commitment to honest, open inquiry, and to clear communication of any research aims, sponsorship, social context, personal values, or financial interests that might affect or appear to affect the research.

III.20   Submit their research, in some accurate form and within the limits of confidentiality, to persons with expertise in the research area, for their comments and evaluations, prior to publication or the preparation of any final report.

III.21   Encourage and not interfere with the free and open exchange of psychological knowledge and theory between themselves, their students, colleagues, and the public.

III.22   Make no attempt to conceal the status of a trainee and, if a trainee is providing direct client service, ensure that the client is informed of that fact.

Avoidance of incomplete disclosure

III.23   Not engage in incomplete disclosure, or in temporarily leading research participants to believe that a research project or some aspect of it has a different purpose, if there are alternative procedures available or if the negative effects cannot be predicted or offset.

III.24   Not engage in incomplete disclosure, or in temporarily leading research participants to believe that a research project or some aspect of it has a different purpose, if it would interfere with the person's understanding of facts that clearly might influence a decision to give adequately informed consent (e.g., withholding information about the level of risk, discomfort, or inconvenience).

III.25   Use the minimum necessary incomplete disclosure or temporary leading of research participants to believe that a research project or some aspect of it has a different purpose, when such research procedures are used.

III.26   Debrief research participants as soon as possible after the participants' involvement, if there has been incomplete disclosure or temporary leading of research participants to believe that a research project or some aspect of it has a different purpose.

III.27   Provide research participants, during such debriefing, with a clarification of the nature of the study, seek to remove any misconceptions that might have arisen, and seek to re-establish any trust that might have been lost, assuring the participants that the research procedures were neither arbitrary nor capricious, but necessary for scientifically valid findings. (Also see Standards II.23 and II.44.)

III.28   Act to re-establish with research participants any trust that might have been lost due to the use of incomplete disclosure or temporarily leading research participants to believe that the research project or some aspect of it had a different purpose.

III.29   Give a research participant the option of removing his or her data, if the research participant expresses concern during the debriefing about the incomplete disclosure or the temporary leading of the research participant to believe that the research project or some aspect of it had a different purpose, and if removal of the data will not compromise the validity of the research design and hence diminish the ethical value of the participation of the other research participants.

III.30   Seek an independent and adequate ethical review of the risks to public or individual trust and of safeguards to protect such trust for any research that plans to provide incomplete disclosure or temporarily lead research participants to believe that the research project or some aspect of it has a different purpose, before making a decision to proceed.

Avoidance of conflict of interest

III.31   Not exploit any relationship established as a psychologist to further personal, political, or business interests at the expense of the best interests of their clients, research participants, students, employers, or others. This includes, but is not limited to: soliciting clients of one's employing agency for private practice; taking advantage of trust or dependency to encourage or engage in sexual intimacies (e.g., with clients not included in Standard II.27, with clients' partners or relatives, with students or trainees not included in Standard II.28, or with research participants); taking advantage of trust or dependency to frighten clients into receiving services; misappropriating students' ideas, research or work; using the resources of one's employing institution for purposes not agreed to; giving or receiving kickbacks or bonuses for referrals; seeking or accepting loans or investments from clients; and, prejudicing others against a colleague for reasons of personal gain.

III.32   Not offer rewards sufficient to motivate an individual or group to participate in an activity that has possible or known risks to themselves or others. (Also see Standards I.27, I.28, II.2, and II.49.)

III.33   Avoid dual or multiple relationships (e.g., with clients, research participants, employees, supervisees, students, or trainees) and other situations that might present a conflict of interest or that might reduce their ability to be objective and unbiased in their determinations of what might be in the best interests of others.

III.34   Manage dual or multiple relationships that are unavoidable due to cultural norms or other circumstances in such a manner that bias, lack of objectivity, and risk of exploitation are minimized. This might include obtaining ongoing supervision or consultation for the duration of the dual or multiple relationship, or involving a third party in obtaining consent (e.g., approaching a client or employee about becoming a research participant).

III.35   Inform all parties, if a real or potential conflict of interest arises, of the need to resolve the situation in a manner that is consistent with Respect for the Dignity of Persons (Principle I) and Responsible Caring (Principle II), and take all reasonable steps to resolve the issue in such a manner.

Reliance on the discipline

III.36   Familiarize themselves with their discipline's rules and regulations, and abide by them, unless abiding by them would be seriously detrimental to the rights or welfare of others as demonstrated in the Principles of Respect for the Dignity of Persons or Responsible Caring. (See Standards IV.17 and IV.18 for guidelines regarding the resolution of such conflicts.)

III.37   Familiarize themselves with and demonstrate a commitment to maintaining the standards of their discipline.

III.38   Seek consultation from colleagues and/or appropriate groups and committees, and give due regard to their advice in arriving at a responsible decision, if faced with difficult situations.

Extended responsibility

III.39   Encourage others, in a manner consistent with this Code, to relate with integrity.

III.40   Assume overall responsibility for the scientific and professional activities of their assistants, employees, supervisees, students, and trainees with regard to the Principle of Integrity in Relationships, all of whom, however, incur similar obligations.

PRINCIPLE IV:
RESPONSIBILITY TO SOCIETY

Values Statement

Psychology functions as a discipline within the context of human society.[4] Psychologists, both in their work and as private citizens, have responsibilities to the societies in which they live and work, such as the neighbourhood or city, and to the welfare of all human beings in those societies.

Two of the legitimate expectations of psychology as a science and a profession are that it will increase knowledge and that it will conduct its affairs in such ways that it will promote the welfare of all human beings.

Freedom of enquiry and debate (including scientific and academic freedom) is a foundation of psychological education, science, and practice. In the context of society, the above expectations imply that psychologists will exercise this freedom through the use of activities and methods that are consistent with ethical requirements.

The above expectations also imply that psychologists will do whatever they can to ensure that psychological knowledge, when used in the development of social structures and policies, will be used for beneficial purposes, and that the discipline's own structures and policies will support those beneficial purposes. Within the context of this document, social structures and policies that have beneficial purposes are defined as those that more readily support and reflect respect for the dignity of persons, responsible caring, integrity in relationships, and responsibility to society. If psychological knowledge or structures are used against these purposes, psychologists have an ethical responsibility to try to draw attention to and correct the misuse. Although this is a collective responsibility, those psychologists having direct involvement in the structures of the discipline, in social development, or in the theoretical or research data base that is being used (e.g., through research, expert testimony, or policy advice) have the greatest responsibility to act. Other psychologists must decide for themselves the most appropriate and beneficial use of their time and talents to help meet this collective responsibility.

In carrying out their work, psychologists acknowledge that many social structures have evolved slowly over time in response to human need and are valued by the societies that have developed them. In such circumstances, psychologists convey respect for such social structures

---

4   Society is used here in the broad sense of a group of persons living as members of one or more human communities, rather than in the limited sense of state or government.

and avoid unwarranted or unnecessary disruption. Suggestions for and action toward changes or enhancement of such structures are carried out through processes that seek to achieve a consensus within those societies and/or through democratic means.

On the other hand, if structures or policies seriously ignore or oppose the principles of respect for the dignity of persons, responsible caring, integrity in relationships, or responsibility to society, psychologists involved have a responsibility to speak out in a manner consistent with the principles of this Code, and advocate for appropriate change to occur as quickly as possible.

In order to be responsible and accountable to society, and to contribute constructively to its ongoing development, psychologists need to be willing to work in partnership with others, be self-reflective, and be open to external suggestions and criticisms about the place of the discipline of psychology in society. They need to engage in even-tempered observation and interpretation of the effects of societal structures and policies, and their process of change, developing the ability of psychologists to increase the beneficial use of psychological knowledge and structures, and avoid their misuse. The discipline needs to be willing to set high standards for its members, to do what it can to assure that such standards are met, and to support its members in their attempts to maintain the standards. Once again, individual psychologists must decide for themselves the most appropriate and beneficial use of their time and talents in helping to meet these collective responsibilities.

Ethical Standards
In adhering to the Principle of Responsibility to Society, psychologists would:

Development of knowledge
IV.1   Contribute to the discipline of psychology and of society's understanding of itself and human beings generally, through free enquiry and the acquisition, transmission, and expression of knowledge and ideas, unless such activities conflict with other basic ethical requirements.

IV.2   Not interfere with, or condone interference with, free enquiry and the acquisition, transmission, and expression of knowledge and ideas that do not conflict with other basic ethical requirements.

IV.3   Keep informed of progress in their area(s) of psychological activity, take this progress into account in their work, and try to make their own contributions to this progress.

Beneficial activities

IV.4   Participate in and contribute to continuing education and the professional and scientific growth of self and colleagues.

IV.5   Assist in the development of those who enter the discipline of psychology by helping them to acquire a full understanding of their ethical responsibilities, and the needed competencies of their chosen area(s), including an understanding of critical analysis and of the variations, uses, and possible misuses of the scientific paradigm.

IV.6   Participate in the process of critical self-evaluation of the discipline's place in society, and in the development and implementation of structures and procedures that help the discipline to contribute to beneficial societal functioning and changes.

IV.7   Provide and/or contribute to a work environment that supports the respectful expression of ethical concern or dissent, and the constructive resolution of such concern or dissent.

IV.8   Engage in regular monitoring, assessment, and reporting (e.g., through peer review, and in programme reviews, case management reviews, and reports of one's own research) of their ethical practices and safeguards.

IV.9   Help develop, promote, and participate in accountability processes and procedures related to their work.

IV.10   Uphold the discipline's responsibility to society by promoting and maintaining the highest standards of the discipline.

IV.11   Protect the skills, knowledge, and interpretations of psychology from being misused, used incompetently, or made useless (e.g., loss of security of assessment techniques) by others.

IV.12   Contribute to the general welfare of society (e.g., improving accessibility of services, regardless of ability to pay) and/or to the general welfare of their discipline, by offering a portion of their time to work for which they receive little or no financial return.

IV.13   Uphold the discipline's responsibility to society by bringing incompetent or unethical behaviour, including misuses of psychological knowledge and techniques, to the attention of appropriate authorities, committees, or regulatory bodies, in a manner consistent with the ethical principles of this Code, if informal resolution or correction of the situation is not appropriate or possible.

IV.14   Enter only into agreements or contracts that allow them to act in accordance with the ethical principles and standards of this Code.

Respect for society

IV.15 Acquire an adequate knowledge of the culture, social structure, and customs of a community before beginning any major work there.

IV.16 Convey respect for and abide by prevailing community mores, social customs, and cultural expectations in their scientific and professional activities, provided that this does not contravene any of the ethical principles of this Code.

IV.17 Familiarize themselves with the laws and regulations of the societies in which they work, especially those that are related to their activities as psychologists, and abide by them. If those laws or regulations seriously conflict with the ethical principles contained herein, psychologists would do whatever they could to uphold the ethical principles. If upholding the ethical principles could result in serious personal consequences (e.g., jail or physical harm), decision for final action would be considered a matter of personal conscience.

IV.18 Consult with colleagues, if faced with an apparent conflict between abiding by a law or regulation and following an ethical principle, unless in an emergency, and seek consensus as to the most ethical course of action and the most responsible, knowledgeable, effective, and respectful way to carry it out.

Development of society

IV.19 Act to change those aspects of the discipline of psychology that detract from beneficial societal changes, where appropriate and possible.

IV.20 Be sensitive to the needs, current issues, and problems of society, when determining research questions to be asked, services to be developed, content to be taught, information to be collected, or appropriate interpretation of results or findings.

IV.21 Be especially careful to keep well informed of social issues through relevant reading, peer consultation, and continuing education, if their work is related to societal issues.

IV.22 Speak out, in a manner consistent with the four principles of this Code, if they possess expert knowledge that bears on important societal issues being studied or discussed.

IV.23 Provide thorough discussion of the limits of their data with respect to social policy, if their work touches on social policy and structure.

IV.24 Consult, if feasible and appropriate, with groups, organizations, or communities being studied, in order to increase the accuracy of interpretation of results and to minimize risk of misinterpretation or misuse.

IV.25 Make themselves aware of the current social and political climate and of previous and possible future societal misuses of psychological knowledge, and exercise due discretion in communicating psychological information (e.g., research results, theoretical knowledge), in order to discourage any further misuse.

IV.26 Exercise particular care when reporting the results of any work regarding vulnerable groups, ensuring that results are not likely to be misinterpreted or misused in the development of social policy, attitudes, and practices (e.g., encouraging manipulation of vulnerable persons or reinforcing discrimination against any specific population).

IV.27 Not contribute to nor engage in research or any other activity that contravenes international humanitarian law, such as the development of methods intended for use in the torture of persons, the development of prohibited weapons, or destruction of the environment.

IV.28 Provide the public with any psychological knowledge relevant to the public's informed participation in the shaping of social policies and structures, if they possess expert knowledge that bears on the social policies and structures.

IV.29 Speak out and/or act, in a manner consistent with the four principles of this Code, if the policies, practices, laws, or regulations of the social structure within which they work seriously ignore or contradict any of the principles of this Code.

Extended responsibility

IV.30 Encourage others, in a manner consistent with this Code, to exercise responsibility to society.

IV.31 Assume overall responsibility for the scientific and professional activities of their assistants, employees, supervisees, students, and trainees with regard to the Principle of Responsibility to Society, all of whom, however, incur similar obligations.

Canadian Psychological Association Practice Guidelines for Providers of Psychological Services

Practice guidelines for psychologists who provide psychological services serve the important purpose of describing professional activities which demonstrate compliance with the profession's standards of ethical and competent behaviour. The Canadian Psychological Association provides this revision of its policy document Standards for Providers of Psychological Services (1978) pursuant to the adoption of the Canadian Code of Ethics for Psychologists (March, 1986). This revision of the guidelines is cross referenced to current standards documents, including the Canadian Code of Ethics for Psychologists, (1991).[1] The objectives of the guidelines for the providers of psychological services and for the users of such services include the following:

- Practice guidelines define common expectations for organizations and psychologists who provide psychological services and for the user of the service. They provide both the provider and the user with a baseline or criteria for evaluating the quality and appropriateness of practice.
- Practice guidelines provide an external authority for standards of ethical and competent practice for psychologists working in situations where others may be minimally knowledgeable and minimally supportive of these standards. Situations when such

---

1 This reprint of *Canadian Psychological Association Practice Guidelines for Providers of Psychological Services* has been updated by changing all cross-references to the 2000 Code. The original printing (1989) was cross-referenced to the 1986 Code and the second printing (1992) was cross-referenced to the 1991 Code.

guidelines may be helpful may arise in working within organizational structures, or with third-party users.

- Practice guidelines have significant influence on tomorrow's professionals through their incorporation into teaching models.
- Practice guidelines may contribute toward legislative and regulatory requirement for the practice of psychology. Guidelines may assist in providing greater legislative uniformity across Canada with regard to standards of training, qualifications, and competence.
- Practice guidelines may give specific content and structure to the profession's principles of ethical practice.

There are a number of features of the following practice guidelines for psychologists that warrant attention. *First*, guidelines identify standards of behaviour and approaches to service delivery which must be provided to at least a minimal level across the full range of psychological services. However, psychologists are expected to strive for excellence in the practice of their profession. *Second*, in order to assist psychologists in identifying the underlying principles, the practice guidelines are cross referenced to ethical principles and standards in the 3rd edition of the Canadian Code of Ethics for Psychologists (2000). However, the practice guidelines are not seen as a substitute for the Code. The practice guidelines are based on the Code, and are not intended to provide comprehensive coverage of the Code, nor of the professional ideals and models for ethical decision making contained within the Code. *Third*, if these guidelines are used in the context of quality assurance mechanisms, they may help to safeguard the public and provide a context within which service innovations may be safely made. These guidelines should not constrain psychologists from employing new methods or making flexible use of innovative procedures in serving the public and increasing the body of psychological knowledge. *Fourth*, it is believed that all Canadian psychologists in professional practice should be guided by a common code of ethics. While it is recognized that provincial regulatory bodies adopt their own enforceable standards documents, the Canadian Psychological Association's guidelines can provide leadership, information, and inspiration in a manner which is designed to complement the work of provincial jurisdictions.

Standards evolve over time. The following sets of standards were reviewed in the preparation of this document:

- The Canadian Psychological Association Standards for Providers of Psychological Services (1978).
- The American Psychological Association Standards for Providers of Psychological Services (1977, 1987).

- The Canadian Psychological Association Canadian Code of Ethics for Psychologists (1986, 1991, 2000). (CCE).
- Provincial minimum practice standards adopted between 1978 and 1989.

The guidelines are divided into several sections, beginning with definitions of the terms to be used. Five general areas of standards follow, these being:

    I. Provision of service.
    II. Organization of services.
    III. Client relationships.
    IV. Training, qualifications and competence.
    V. Record keeping.

DEFINITIONS

Providers of psychological services refers to:

- Professional psychologist practitioners who are registered/certified/licensed in a province/territory where psychology is regulated by statute, and who may work independently or may be employed in a larger organizational unit.
- Any other persons who offer psychological services under the supervision of a professional psychologist.
- Professional psychologist administrators who are responsible for organized psychological services units including agencies, departments, programs, teams, or other types of units.
- A larger organization which mandates, funds, and/or employs staff to provide psychological services as part of its overall operations.

Psychological services refers to one or more of the following:

- Evaluation, diagnosis, and assessment of the functioning of individuals and/or groups in a variety of settings and activities.
- Interventions to facilitate the functioning of individuals and groups.
- Consultation relating to the assessment of the functioning of individuals or interventions to facilitate the functioning of individuals and groups.
- Programme development of services in the areas identified above.
- Supervision of psychological services.

A *psychological service unit* is the functional unit through which psychological services are provided. This includes, but is not limited to, the following:

- A unit which provides predominantly psychological services and is composed of one or more professional psychologists and supporting staff.
- A psychological service unit which operates as a professional service or as a functional or geographic component of a larger governmental, educational, correctional, health-related, training, industrial or commercial organizational unit.
- A psychologist providing professional services in a multi-occupational setting.
- An individual or group of individuals in a private practice or a psychological consulting firm.

Clients or users of psychological services refers to all clients, irrespective of age or presenting problem and includes individuals, groups, families, organizations or whole ecologies of human beings and their institutions. (APA, 1987). Users/clients include, but are not limited to, the following:

- Direct users or recipients of psychological services.
- Public and private institutions, facilities, or organizations receiving psychological services.
- Third-party purchasers of psychological services. This includes purchasers who pay for delivery of services, but who may not be the recipients of those services.

I. PROVISION OF SERVICES

1.1. Psychologists design the content and form of psychological services to meet the needs of users.

a. The psychologist administrators of service units systematically collect and analyze information on the needs of users in order to develop appropriate service programs. They identify which user interests are addressed by the program. (CCE II. 13, 14)

b. The psychologist practitioners assess individual user/client needs and assure that individual services are suited to these needs before the services are provided. (CCE II. 13, 14)

c. The psychologist practitioners recognize that when there is conflict between employer or third party user need and that of the direct recipient client need, that the latter takes priority. (CCE I. Values Statement; 1.26)

1.2.   The psychologist administrators are responsible for assuring the psychologist practitioners are suitably trained in the skills and techniques necessary for providing the services offered.

   a. The psychologist administrators of service units which offer a wide or diverse range of services assure that the psychologist practitioners concentrate on specific areas of practice or competence, and do not offer a range of services so broad as to reduce or dilute expertise. (CCE II.6, 8)

   b. The psychologist administrators of service units assure that psychologist practitioners have sufficient diversity of training and experience to meet diverse service needs. (CCE II.6, 25)

   c. The psychologist administrators assure that persons performing psychological service functions who do not meet standards for professional practice are supervised by professional psychologists with appropriate training and experience. (CCE I.47; II.7, 50; III.40; IV.31)

1.3.   All levels of providers of psychological services are responsible for providing services efficiently and effectively.

   a. Psychologist practitioners are responsible to only offer services for which they have established their competence, or to obtain adequate supervision when extending their areas of competence to new areas. (CCE II.6, 8)

   b. Agencies, psychologist administrators and practitioners work to ensure that users receive services in a timely fashion. Psychologists take action to avoid waiting periods or delays in the provision of services by monitoring the volume of service requests, and the capability of meeting those demands. Options for avoiding unreasonable delays may include increasing the number of psychologists in a service unit, establishing a hierarchy of user needs, or directing users to alternate services. (CCE II.1, 2, 13, 22, 31; IV.9)

   c. All levels of providers of psychological services monitor, review, or evaluate the effectiveness of services to ensure that user needs are met. Providers may alter or revise services to ensure effectiveness. They may adopt more effective new or alternate services as they become available. (CCE II.1, 21, 22; IV.3, 9)

   d. Psychologists are accountable for the services that they provide to the users of the service, and may also be accountable where applicable to an employer, to an external accrediting body, and to their professional regulator body. Psychologists actively participate in procedures established by the employer or the profession of psychology for the purpose of review and evaluation of psychological practice. Psychologists ensure that these procedures comply with the standards of the Code of Ethics. Professional standards and guidelines for psychological practice are used to evaluate the quality of service delivery, and provide a basis for corrective action when deficiencies are discovered. (CCE II.3, 22, 37: III.37; IV.6, 8, 9, 10)

II. ORGANIZATION OF SERVICES

II.1.   Psychologists establish the rationale and philosophy of services through clear statements of service delivery objectives.

 a. The psychologist administrators organize professional services to meet stated objectives that identify the intended recipients and the general nature of the services to be provided. (CCE II. 18; III.5)

 b. Professional service program objectives are consistent with meeting the needs and well-being of users of psychological services. (CCE II.1, 13)

 c. Psychologist practitioners negotiate individual client objectives to meet the needs and well-being of individual users. (CCE I.16, 17; II.1, 49)

 d. Psychologists communicate professional service objectives to staff, users, and other disciplines. (CCE III.5; IV.9)

II.2.   Psychologists develop clearly defined policies and procedures to structure the delivery of services.

 a. Psychologists within psychological service units adopt written procedures and policies that are consistent with professional standards for competent and ethical practice. (CCE IV.10, 14)

 b. Psychologists inform clients of the procedures and policies that govern the provision of service. (CCE III.14, 16)

 c. Psychologists develop procedures and policies that are consistent with codes of ethics and with standards established by professional regulatory bodies. (CCE III.36, 37; IV.10)

II.3.   Psychologists establish clear lines of professional responsibility and accountability.

 a. Supervisory and professional roles and relationships within psychological service units are clearly defined. (CCE I.47; II.25, 50; III.14, 40; IV.9, 31)

 b. A professional psychologist directs and administers a psychological service unit. (CCE I.47; II.50; III.40; IV.31)

c. Supervisors must accept a special responsibility to protect the interests of both users and providers of services in those situations where the persons providing the services do not have current professional accreditation in psychology. (CCE 1.47; II.1, 2, 3, 7, 25, 49, 50)

d. Psychologists in a service unit provide regular, systematic evaluation of services at the organizational level. (CCE II.22; IV.8, 9)

e. Psychologists in a service unit monitor the adequacy of their staffing patterns to meet service demands and seek to redress staffing shortages that create barriers to service delivery. (CCE II.1, 22; IV.9)

III. CLIENT RELATIONSHIPS

III.1. Psychologists strive to make their client relationships clear and unambiguous.

a. Psychologists discuss with their clients the nature of their relationship, and clarify any factors that bear upon that relationship. They clarify limits to confidentiality of psychological records and, if there is a third-party payer for the services, they inform the client of the nature and extent of details that may be released to the third party (e.g., insurance companies, lawyers, courts). (CCE 1.23, 24, 26; III.14)

b. Psychologists avoid dual relationships with clients and/or relationships that might impair their professional judgment or increase the risk of client exploitation. Examples of dual relationships include treating employees, supervisors, close friends or relatives. Sexual relations with clients are prohibited. (CCE II.27; III.31, 33)

c. Psychologists faced with making difficult ethical decisions seek professional consultation and support (CCE 1.31; III.30, 34, 38; IV.18)

III.2. Psychologists only use advertising or marketing strategies, and only make public statements, that are consistent with the welfare of the client, other psychologists, and of the profession of psychology. (CCE 1.1, 2, 30; III.2, 5, 8, 9, 31)

a. To ensure that advertising and marketing strategies are targeted toward appropriate potential users, psychologists provide services to clients only if the service is based upon sound psychological principles or established research findings. (CCE II.9, 21)

b. Psychologists use only those advertising and marketing approaches that are based upon sound business principles and that reflect well on the profession of psychology. Claims made by psychologists shall be based upon sound research findings, and may not employ testimonials, selective survey results, or misleading or false information. (CCE III.1, 2, 5, 8)

c. Psychologists who interpret the science and practice of psychology to the public enter into a relationship with the public users of that information. Psychologists base public statements upon fact and established information and do not make public statements in areas where they do not possess expertise. Psychologists clearly differentiate between statements that are supported by empirical evidence and those which are based on opinion. (CCE III.11, 13; IV.20, 23, 25, 26)

III.3. Psychologists set reasonable fees for the services they render, inform the client of the fees that will apply to them, and collect fees in a manner that is considerate of the welfare of the client. Psychologists inform clients about fees and fee collection methods as early in the relationship as possible. (CCE I.15, 23; II.1; III.14, 31)

IV. TRAINING, QUALIFICATIONS AND COMPETENCE

IV.1. Psychologists practice within the limits of their competence. Psychologists obtain training in the special areas of expertise where they will provide services. The training must meet the criteria for independent practice as required by the appropriate provincial/territorial regulatory body. Such training may include formal course work, research, individual study, applied training and/or supervision as deemed appropriate. (CCE II.6, 8, 9; III.4, 36, 37)

IV.2. Psychologists who provide services maintain current knowledge of scientific and professional developments that are directly related to the services they render. (CCE II.9; IV.4)

IV.3. Psychologists who wish to change their specialized area of practice, or wish to expand their areas of competence, obtain such training as required by the provincial regulatory body. (CCE II.6; III.4,36, 37)

IV.4. Psychologists maintain knowledge of specialized standards and qualifications that are necessary in the areas in which they provide service. Where necessary and/or appropriate, psychologists obtain special training in the areas in which they provide service, and observe the standards for providers of those services. (CCE II,6, 8, 9; III.4, 36, 37; IV.10)

IV.5. Psychologists do not provide services when their ability to do so is impaired by alcohol, drugs, physical or psychological disturbance, or other dysfunction. (CCE II.10, 11, 12)

a. Providers who deem themselves, or are deemed to be, unable to provide services ensure that their clients are not adversely affected. Clients are informed of the inability to provide services and, where necessary and/or appropriate, are referred to other service providers. (CCE II.21, 31)

V. RECORD KEEPING AND CONFIDENTIALITY

V.1. Psychologists maintain accurate and current records of services provided.

a. Psychologists maintain records with sufficient information for monitoring and evaluating the services provided. (CCE II.19, 22)

b. Psychologists respect clients' privacy by collecting and recording only that information necessary to respond to the needs of the client with appropriate services. When records are used for purposes not directly related to service provision, providers establish policies for protecting the rights of clients and their privacy, and for ensuring that information from records is not used in a manner that violates their rights and privacy. (CCE 1.37–42, 45, 46)

c. Psychologists respect clients' rights of access to their own records and they develop procedures to permit user access and user correction of errors. (CCE 1.8; III.15; IV. 17)

V.2. All levels of providers work to establish and maintain a reliable method for safekeeping and control of records.

a. Psychologists control access to psychological service records regardless of the method of storage (e.g. physical, electronic, etc.). When records from a psychological service unit are made part of an organization-wide record-keeping system, psychologists develop procedural safeguards to ensure control over the part of the record collected by the provider of psychological service. (CCE 1.41, 42)

b. All levels of providers ensure the physical safety of records from loss or damage. Information stored electronically is duplicated so that restoration after accidental loss or damage of an original version is possible. (CCE 1.41, 42) v.3.   All levels of providers establish unequivocal procedures for releasing records only with the fully informed consent of users.

   a. Psychologists inform users of any limits to confidentiality of information concerning them, such as access to records or service information required by third-party users or courts. (CCE 1.24, 26, 44, 45; III.14)

   b. Psychologists safeguard the confidentiality of information released to third parties, by providing suitable advice to recipients about the confidential nature of the information. (CE 1.7; II.5)

   c. Psychologists avoid releasing information that requires professional training for interpretation or analysis to persons who lack that training. When this information must or should be released, providers advise recipients about the limits to the usefulness or meaningfulness of the information. (CCE 1.7; II.2, 15, 30; III.8)

   d. Psychologists are cognizant of legally established limits on confidentiality that apply in the jurisdictions in which they deliver psychological services. These limits are addressed, whenever appropriate, within the informed consent procedure which is an integral component of a psychological service. (CCE 1.24, 26, 45; IV.17)

Canadian Psychological Association Guidelines For Non-discriminatory Practice

PREAMBLE

These guidelines were developed to encourage non-discriminatory practice among psychologists. They were based on the Canadian Code of Ethics for Psychologists (CPA, 1991) and have been updated to cross reference to the third edition of the Code (CPA, 2000).[1] The guidelines are aspirational in intent. The goal is to promote non-discriminatory care in therapeutic work with clients, as well as to provide guidelines for evaluating the extent to which one's work falls within the parameters of non-discriminatory practice. As our society and culture become more diverse, and as we become more aware of specific diversities, it is important that psychologists gain an awareness of the need for non-discriminatory practice. As the need arises, guidelines can be developed for use of specific diversities.

ETHICAL PRINCIPLES APPLIED TO NON-DISCRIMINATORY PRACTICE

Principle 1: Respect for the Dignity of Persons

The principle of Respect for the Dignity of Persons (CPA, 2000) requires psychologists in practice, teaching and research to actively

---

1 These guidelines were prepared and updated by Sharon Crozier, Susan Harris, Carolyn Larsen, Jean Pettifor, and Lynne Sloan, with the assistance of the Committee on Ethics of the Canadian Psychological Association.

demonstrate a belief that each person should be treated primarily as a person or an end in him/herself, not as an object or a means to an end. Psychologists appreciate that the innate worth of human beings is not enhanced or reduced by their culture, nationality, ethnicity, colour, race, religion, sex, gender, marital status, sexual orientation, physical or mental abilities, age, socioeconomic status, or any other preference or personal characteristic, condition, or status. Psychologists also recognize that as individual, family, group, or community vulnerabilities increase, or as the power of persons to control their environment or their lives decreases, psychologists have an increasing responsibility to seek ethical advice and to establish safeguards to protect the rights of those less able to protect themselves. These responsibilities have special significance in a society which is becoming more diverse culturally and economically and which has not achieved gender equality. In addition to specific non-discriminatory practices, special care must be taken in providing for free and informed consent, respecting privacy, and clarifying the protection and limitations on confidentiality. Psychologists do not impose the dominant culture world view on those who are different. Psychologists continually monitor how they demonstrate respect when working with diverse populations.

Principle II: Responsible Caring

The principle of Responsible Caring (CPA, 2000) requires psychologists to demonstrate an active concern for the welfare of all individuals, groups, and communities with whom they relate in their role as psychologists. There is an additional responsibility to take care that persons in vulnerable positions have equal access to the benefits of psychological knowledge and services. Psychologists recognize the impact of society in creating and maintaining the problems and issues faced by persons who are perceived as different from the norm of mainstream society. Psychologists are committed to the belief that all persons are of equal worth. Psychologists are interested in empowering vulnerable persons so that they have equal opportunities in mainstream society, recognizing that in addition to personal coping skills this requires political and social changes. Psychologists are particularly cognizant of power differentials in society that discriminate against diverse populations. Responsible caring addresses the immediate short-term and long-term welfare of others.

Psychologists recognize that, in order to adequately care for the welfare of others, especially for the welfare of those who are vulnerable, dependent, or suffer oppression and discrimination in society, they need to be competent in their activities as psychologists. Competence requires specific knowledge, skills and attitudes used for the benefit of others. Competence also requires self-monitoring of one's own knowledge base, personal values, experiences, biases, attitudes, and socialization, which influence how they practice. Psychologists also act to maintain their level of competence. Providing incompetent services places others at risk of harm.

Principle III: Integrity in Relationships

The principle of Integrity in Relationships (CPA, 2000) requires that psychologists be honest, open, objective and accurate in all their activities as psychologists. They avoid dishonesty, deception, bias, and inaccuracy. The individual characteristics, values and beliefs of psychologists influence the questions they ask and the assumptions, observations, and interpretations they make. Psychologists are responsible for managing situations where conflicts arise between their own personal, political, or business interests and the interests of others. Integrity in relationships can easily be compromised when working with diverse populations, especially with groups that may be generally devalued in society.

Principle IV: Responsibility to Society

The Principle of Responsibility to Society (CPA, 2000) requires that psychologists demonstrate a concern for the welfare of all human beings in society. They may choose for themselves the most appropriate and beneficial use of their time and talents to help meet this collective responsibility. There are multiple avenues for social action. A discipline that maintains high standards for its members is serving the interests of society. Knowledge may be used to influence social policy. Public education, advocacy, and lobbying are appropriate. If social policy and societal attitudes seriously ignore or violate the ethical principles of respect, caring and honesty to the harm of special populations, then psychologists have a responsibility to be critical and to advocate for change to occur as quickly as possible. There is social injustice when segments of society are devalued or oppressed. In a society that is increasingly diverse, there is increasing potential for injustice. To the extent that individuals and groups without power suffer oppression in our imperfect society, psychologists have an ethical responsibility to use their knowledge and power to contribute to social change.

GUIDELINES FOR ETHICAL PRACTICE WITH DIVERSE POPULATIONS

1. Recognize the inherent worth of all human beings regardless of how different they may be from oneself.
2. Be aware of one's own cultural, moral, and social beliefs, and be sensitive to how they may enhance one's interactions with others or may interfere with promoting the welfare of others.
3. Recognize the power differential between oneself and others in order to diminish the differences, and to use power for the advantage of others rather than unwittingly to abuse it.
4. Study group or cultural norms in order to recognize individual differences within the larger context.
5. Be aware that theories or precepts developed to describe people from the dominant culture may apply differently to people from non-dominant cultures.
6. Recognize the reality, variety, and implications of all forms of oppression in society, and facilitate clients' examination of options in dealing with such experiences.
7. Recognize that those who are subjected to physical or sexual assault are victims of crime, and that those who assault are guilty of crimes.
8. Be knowledgeable about community resources available for diverse populations.
9. Respect, listen and learn from clients who are different from oneself in order to understand what is in their best interests.
10. Use inclusive and respectful language.
11. Share all relevant decision making with clients including goals of the interaction and the nature of proposed interventions in order to serve their best interests.
12. Ensure that consent is truly informed, keeping in mind diversity issues and cultural differences.
13. Be especially careful to be open, honest, and straightforward, remembering that persons who are oppressed may be distrustful or overly trustful of those in authority.
14. Assess accurately the source of difficulties, apportioning causality appropriately between individual, situational, and cultural factors.
15. Respect privacy and confidentiality according to the wishes of clients, and explain fully any limitations on confidentiality which may exist.
16. Evaluate the cultural meaning of dual/multiple and overlapping relationships in order to show respect and to avoid exploitation.

17. Constantly reevaluate one's competence, attitudes, and effectiveness in working with diverse populations.
18. Consult with others who may be more familiar with diversity in order to provide competent services.
19. Acknowledge one's own vulnerabilities and care for oneself outside of relationships as psychologists.
20. Make competent services available to disadvantaged groups by offering services at a lower cost in proportion to the client's income for a proportion of one's caseload.
21. Choose ways in which one can contribute to the making of a society that is respectful and caring of all its citizens.

APPENDIX D

Regulators and Associations

INTERNATIONAL

Association of State and Provincial
Psychology Boards (ASPPB)
P.O. Box 241245
Montgomery, AL
USA   36124–1245

Telephone: (334) 832–4580
E-mail: asppb@asppb.org
Web site: www. asppb.org

NATIONAL

Canadian Psychological Association (CPA)
151 Slater St., Suite 205
Ottawa, ON KIP 5H3

Telephone: (613) 237–2144/
          1–888–472–0657
Facsimile: (613) 237–1674
E-mail: cpamemb@cpa.ca
Web site: www. cpa.ca

Canadian Register of Health Service
Providers in Psychology (CRHSPP)
368 Dalhousie St., Suite 300
Ottawa, ON KIN 5P4

Telephone: (613) 562–0900
Facsimile: (613) 562–0902
E-mail: info@ crhspp.ca
Web site: www. crhspp.ca

PROVINCIAL AND TERRITORIAL

Alberta

College of Alberta Psychologists
2100 SunLife Place,
10123–99 St.
Edmonton, AB T5J 3H1

Telephone: (780) 424–5070
Facsimile: (780) 420–1241
E-mail: psych@cap.ab.ca
Web site: www.cap.ab.ca

Psychologists Association of Alberta
Suite 520, Metropolitan Place
10303 Jasper Ave.
Edmonton, AB T5J 3N6

Telephone: (780) 424–0294/
          1–888–424–0297
Facsimile: 1–888–423–4048
E-mail:
paa@psychologistsassociation.ab.ca
Web site:
www.psychologistsassociation.ab.ca

British Columbia

College of Psychologists of British Columbia
Suite 404
1755 West Broadway
Vancouver, BC V6J 4S5

Telephone: (604) 736-6164
Facsimile: (604) 736-6133
E-mail: cpbc@istar.ca
Web site:
www.collegeofpsychologists.bc.ca

British Columbia Psychological Association
Suite 202
1755 West Broadway
Vancouver, BC V6J 4S5

Telephone: (604) 730-0501/
1-800-730-0522
Facsimile: (604) 730-0502
E-mail: bcpa@interchange.ubc.ca
Web site: www.psychologists.bc.ca

Manitoba

Psychological Association of Manitoba
Suite 253
162-2025 Corydon Ave.
Winnipeg, MB R3P 0N5

Telephone: (204) 487-0784
Facsimile: (204) 487-0784
E-mail: pam@mb.sympatico.ca

Manitoba Psychological Society Inc.
P.O. Box 151
RPO Corydon
Winnipeg, MB R3M 3M7

Telephone: (204) 488-7398
Web site: www.mps.mb.ca

New Brunswick

College of Psychologists of New Brunswick
Suite 211
403 Regent St.
Fredericton, NB E3B 3X6

Telephone: (506) 459-1994
Facsimile: (506) 459-3608
E-mail: cpnb@nbnet.nb.ca
Web site:
http://personal.nbnet.nb.ca/cpnb

Newfoundland

Newfoundland Board of Examiners in Psychology
P.O. Box 5666, Station C
St. John's, NF A1C 5W8

Telephone: (709) 579-6313.
E-mail: jgarlnd@ibm.net

Association of Newfoundland Psychologists
P.O. Box 13700, Station A
St. John's, NF A1B 4G1

Telephone: (709) 739-5405
E-mail: joycen_g@hotmail.com

Northwest Territories

Registrar of Psychologists
Department of Health and Social Services,
Eighth Floor, Centre Square Tower
Government of the NWT
Box 1320
Yellowknife, NT X1A 2L9

Telephone: (867) 920-8637
Facsimile: (867) 873-0484

Association of Psychologists of the
Northwest Territories
Box 1195
Yellowknife, NT X1A 2N8

Telephone: (867) 873–5371 and
(867) 873–8170
E-mail: rbeatch@tamarack.nt.ca

Nova Scotia

Nova Scotia Board of Examiners in
Psychology
Suite 1115, Halifax Professional Centre
5991 Spring Garden Road
Halifax, NS B3H 1Y6

Telephone: (902) 423–2238
Facsimile: (902) 423–0058
E-mail: nsbep@ns.sympatico.ca
Web site:
www3.ns.sympatico.ca/nsbep

Association of Psychologists of Nova
Scotia
P.O. Box 594, Station M
Halifax, NS B3J 2R7

Telephone: (902) 422–9183
E-mail: apns@ns.sympatico.ca
Web site:
http://www3.ns.sympatico.ca/apns

Nunavut

Nunavut Health and Social Services
Government of Nunavut
Box 390
Kugluktuk, NU X0B 0E0

Telephone: (867) 982–7668
Facsimile: (867) 982–3256

Ontario

College of Psychologists of Ontario
Suite 201
1246 Yonge St.
Toronto, ON M4T 1W5

Telephone: (416) 961–8817
Facsimile: (416) 961–2635
Web site: www.cpo.on.ca

Ontario Psychological Association
Suite 221
730 Yonge St.
Toronto, ON M4Y 2B7

Telephone: (416) 961–5552
Facsimile: (416) 961–5516
E-mail: opa@psych.on.ca
Web site: www.psych.on.ca

Prince Edward Island

Prince Edward Island Psychologists
Registration Board
Office of the Dean of Arts
University of Prince Edward Island
Charlottetown, PEI C1A 4P3

Telephone: (902) 566–0307
Facsimile: (902) 566–0304
E-mail: smithp@upei.ca

Prince Edward Island Psychological
Association
Richmond Centre
1 Rochford St.
Charlottetown, PEI C1A 9L2

Telephone: (902) 368–4430
Facsimile: (902) 368–4427

Québec

Ordre des psychologues du Québec
Suite 510
1100 av. Beaumont
Ville Mont Royal, PQ H3P 3E5

Telephone: (514) 738-1881/
               1-800-363-2644
Facsimile: (514) 737-6431
E-mail: sercomm@ordrepsy.qc.ca
Web site: www.ordrepsy.qc.ca

Saskatchewan

Saskatchewan College of Psychologists
348 Albert Street
Regina, SK S4R 2N7

Telephone: (306) 352-1699
Facsimile: (306) 352-1697
E-mail: skcp@sasktel.net
Web site: www.skap.ca

Saskatchewan Psychological Association
P. O. Box 1611
Saskatoon, SK S7K 3R8

Telephone: (306) 352-1699
Facsimile: (306) 352-1697
E-mail: spa@accesscom.ca

Psychological Society of Saskatchewan
Box 4528
Regina, SK S4P 3W7

Facsimile: (306) 766-7888
E-mail: PSS@psychsocietysk.org
Web site: www.psychsocietysk.org

References

A.M. v. Ryan [1997] SCR 157.

Ackerley, G.D., Burnell, J., Holder, D.C., & Kurdek, L.A. (1988). Burnout among licensed psychologists. *Professional Psychology: Research and Practice, 19,* 424–31.

Adelman, H.S., Lusk, R., Alvarez, V., & Acosta, N. K. (1985). Competence of minors to understand, evaluate, and communicate about their psycho-educational problems. *Professional Psychology: Research and Practice, 16,* 426–34.

Association of State and Provincial Psychology Boards. (1990). *Model Rules of Conduct.* Montgomery, AL: Author.

Axelson, J.A. (1993). *Counseling and development in a multicultural society* (2nd ed.). Pacific Grove, CA: Brooks/Cole.

Bass, E. & Davis, L. (1988). *The courage to heal.* New York: Harper & Row.

Bass, L.J., DeMers, S.T., Ogloff, J.R.P., Peterson, C., Pettifor, J.L., Reaves, R.P., Retfalvi, T., Simon, N.P., Sinclair, C., & Tipton, R.M. (1996). *Professional conduct and discipline in psychology.* Washington: American Psychological Association.

Bennett, B.E., Bryant, B.K., VandenBos, G.R., & Greenwood, A. (1990). *Professional liability and risk management.* Washington: American Psychological Association.

Beauchamp, T.L. & Childress, J.F. (2001). *Principles of biomedical ethics.* Oxford: Oxford University Press.

Bois, J.S.A. (1948). The certification of psychologists in Canada. *Canadian Journal of Psychology, 2,* 1–13.

Bouhoutsos, J., Holroyd, J., Lerman, H., Forer, B.R., & Greenberg, M. (1983). Sexual intimacy between psychotherapists and patients. *Professional Psychology: Research and Practice, 14,* 185–96.

Boychyn v. Abbey (2001), O.J. No. 4503.

Brabeck, M.M. (2000). *Practicing feminist ethics in psychology.* Washington: American Psychological Association.

Bram, A.D. (1995). The physically ill or dying psychotherapist: A review of ethical and clinical considerations. *Psychotherapy, 32,* 568–80.

Brown, L.S. (1991). Ethical issues in feminist therapy. *Psychology of Women Quarterly, 15,* 323–36.

Brown, L.S. (1997). The private practice of subversion: Psychology as *tikkun olam*. *American Psychologist, 52*, 449–62.

Cameron, R. & Shepel, L. (1981). Strategies for preserving the confidentiality of psychological reports. *Canadian Psychology, 22*, 191–93.

Canadian Psychological Association. (1986). *CPA policy for agreement between the Canadian Psychological Association and provincial/territorial regulatory bodies and voluntary associations with respect to the investigation and adjudication of complaints regarding professional conduct.* Ottawa: Author.

Canadian Psychological Association. (1988). *Canadian code of ethics for psychologists: Companion manual.* Ottawa: Author.

Canadian Psychological Association. (1990). *Rules and procedures for dealing with ethical complaints.* Ottawa: Author.

Canadian Psychological Association. (2000). *Canadian code of ethics for psychologists* (3rd ed.). Ottawa: Author.

Canadian Psychological Association. (2001). *Guidelines for non-discriminatory practice.* Ottawa: Author.

Canadian Psychological Association. (2001). *Guidelines for psychologists addressing recovered memories.* Ottawa: Author.

Canadian Psychological Association. (2001). *Practice guidelines for providers of psychological services.* Ottawa: Author.

Carnahan v. Coates (1990), 47 B.C.L.R. (2d) 127.

Cassileth, B.R., Zupkins, R.V., Sutton-Smith, K., & March, V. (1980). Informed consent–Why are its goals imperfectly realized? *New England Journal of Medicine, 323*, 896–900.

Catano, V.M. (1994). Application of the CPA code of ethics: Towards integrating the science and practice of psychology. *Canadian Psychology, 35*, 224–28.

Charter of Rights and Freedoms, 46 (as amended) Part I of the Constitution Act, 1982, being schedule B of the Canada Act 1982 (U.K.) 1982, c.11.

Clark, C.R. (1993). Social responsibility ethics: Doing right, doing good, doing well. *Ethics & Behavior, 3*, 303–27.

Coster, J.S. & Schwebel, M. (1997). Well-functioning in professional psychologists. *Professional Psychology: Research and Practice, 28*, 5–13.

Cottone, R.R. & Claus, R.E. (2000). Ethical decision-making models: A review of the literature. *Journal of Counselling & Development, 78*, 275–83.

Cram, S.J. & Dobson, K.S. (1993). Confidentiality: Ethical and legal aspects for Canadian psychologists. *Canadian Psychology, 34*, 347–63.

Criminal Code of Canada, R.S.C. c.C–46 (1985).

Crits v. Sylvester (1956), 1 D.L.R. (2d) 502.

Crowhurst, B. & Dobson, K.S. (1993). Informed consent: Legal issues and applications to clinical practice. *Canadian Psychology, 34*, 329–43.

Daniels, N. (1985). *Just health care.* New York: Columbia University Press.

Dobson, K.S. & Breault, L. (1998). The Canadian Code of Ethics and the regulation of psychology. *Canadian Psychology, 39,* 212–18.

Dobson, K.S. & Dobson, D.J.G. (1993). *Professional psychology in Canada.* Toronto: Hogrefe & Huber.

Dunbar, J. (1998). A critical history of CPA's various codes of ethics for psychologists. *Canadian Psychology, 39,* 177–86.

Edelwich, J. & Brodsky, A. (1991). *Sexual dilemmas for the helping professions* (2nd ed.). New York: Brunner/Mazel.

Evans, D. (1997). *The law, standards of practice, and ethics in the practice of psychology.* Toronto: Emond Montgomery.

Farber, B. (1983). *Stress and burnout in the human service professions.* New York: Pergamon.

Farber, B.A. & Heifetz, L.J. (1982). The process and dimensions of burnout in psychotherapists. *Professional Psychology, 13,* 293–301.

Fowers, B.J. & Richardson, F.C. (1996). Why is multiculturalism good? *American Psychologist, 51,* 609–21.

Gall, G.L. (1995). *The Canadian legal system.* Toronto: Carswell.

Glaser, R.D. & Thorpe, J.S. (1986). Unethical intimacy: A survey of sexual contact and advances between psychology educators and female graduate students. *American Psychologist, 41,* 43–51.

Grisso, T. & Vierling, I. (1978). Minors' consent to treatment: A developmental perspective. *Professional Psychology, 9,* 412–37.

Grosch, W.N. & Olsen, D.C. (1994). *When helping starts to hurt: A new look at burnout among psychotherapists.* New York: W.W. Norton.

Guy, J.D., Poelstra, P.L., & Stark, M.J. (1989). Personal distress and therapeutic effectiveness: National survey of psychologists practicing psychotherapy. *Professional Psychology: Research and Practice, 20,* 48–50.

Guy, J.D. & Souder, J.K. (1986). Impact of therapists' illness or accident on psychotherapeutic practice: Review and discussion. *Professional Psychology: Research and Practice, 17,* 509–13.

Haines v. Bellissimo [1977], 18 O.R. (2d) 177.

Hall v. Hebert [1993] 2 S.C.R. 159.

Hass, L.J. & Malouff, J.L. (1995). *Keeping up the good work: A practitioner's guide to mental health ethics* (2nd ed.). Sarasota, FL: Professional Resource Press.

Hayes, P.A. (1996). Addressing the complexities of culture and gender in counseling. *Journal of Counseling and Development, 74,* 332–38.

Helms, J.E. & Talleyrand, R.M. (1997). Race is not ethnicity. *American Psychologist, 52,* 1246–47.

Hesson, K., Bakal, D., & Dobson, K.S. (1993). Legal and ethical issues concerning children's rights of consent. *Canadian Psychology, 34,* 317–28.

Holroyd, J.C. & Brodsky, A.M. (1977). Psychologists' attitudes and practices regarding erotic and nonerotic physical contact with patients. *American Psychologist, 32*, 843–49.

I.G. v. Rusch (1999), B.C.J. No. 2999.

Ibrahim, F.A. (1996). A multicultural perspective on principle and virtue ethics. *Counseling Psychologist, 24*, 78–85.

Jennings, F.L. (1992). Ethics of rural practice. *Psychotherapy in Private Practice, 10*, 85–104.

Jensen, R. (1979). Competent professional service in psychology: The real issue behind continuing education. *Professional Psychology, 10*, 381–89.

Jones, E.E. (1982). Psychotherapists' impressions of treatment outcome as a function of race. *Journal of Clinical Psychology, 38*, 722–32.

J.S.C. and C.H.C. v. Wren (1986), 76 A.R 115 (Alta. C.A.).

Kant, I. (1959). *Foundations of the metaphysics of morals.* New York: Bobbs-Merrill.

Kaser-Boyd, N., Adelman, H.S., & Taylor, L. (1985). Minors' ability to identify risks and benefits of therapy. *Professional Psychology: Research and Practice, 16*, 411–17.

Keith-Spiegel, P. (1977). Violation of ethical principles due to ignorance or poor professional judgment versus wilful disregard. *Professional Psychology: Research and Practice, 8*, 288–96.

Kelly v. Hazlett (1976), 15 O.R. (2d) 290 (H.C.).

Kitchener, K.S. (1984). Intuition, critical evaluation and ethical principles: The foundation for ethical decision in counseling psychology. *The Counseling Psychologist, 12*, 43–55.

Kluge, E.W. (1992). *Biomedical ethics in a Canadian context.* Scarborough: Prentice-Hall.

Koocher, G.P. (1979). Credentialing in psychology: Close encounters with competence? *American Psychologist, 34*, 696–702.

Laliotis, D.A. & Grayson, J.H. (1985). Psychologist heal thyself: What is available for the impaired psychologist? *American Psychologist, 40*, 84–89.

Lewis, C.C. (1981). How adolescents approach decisions: Changes over grades seven to twelve and policy implications. *Child Development, 52*, 538–44.

M.(A). v. Ryan [1993] 7 W.W.R. 480.

M.(E.) v. Martinson (1993), 81 B.C.L.R. (2d) 184.

Mahoney, M. (1997). Psychotherapists' personal problems and self-care patterns. *Professional Psychology: Research and Practice, 28*, 14–16.

Mann, L., Harmoni, R., & Power, C. (1989). Adolescent decision-making: The development of competence. *Journal of Adolescence, 12*, 265–78.

Maslach, C. (1982). *Burnout, the cost of caring.* Englewood Cliffs: Prentice-Hall.

McInerney v. MacDonald (1992), 12 C.C.L.T. (2d) 255 (SCC).

Merali, N. (1999). Resolution of value conflicts in multicultural counselling. *Canadian Journal of Counselling, 33*, 28–36.

Merali, N. (2002). Culturally informed ethical decision making in situations of suspected child abuse. *Canadian Journal of Counselling, 36*, 233–44.

Mill, J.S. (1833/1985). *John Stuart Mill on politics and society*. Glasgow: William Colins.

Miller, D.J. & Thelen, M.H. (1986). Knowledge and beliefs about confidentiality in psychotherapy. *Professional Psychology: Research and Practice, 17*, 15–19.

N.V. v. Blank (1988), O.J. No. 2544.

Norman, G.R. (1985). Defining competence: A methodological review. In V.R. Neufeld & G.R. Norman (Eds.), *Assessing clinical competence*. New York: Springer.

O'Neill, P. (1989). Responsible to whom? Responsible for what? Some ethical issues in community intervention. *American Journal of Community Psychology, 17*, 323–41.

O'Neill, P. (1998). *Negotiating consent in psychotherapy*. New York: New York University Press.

Overholser, J.C. & Fine, M.A. (1990). Defining the boundaries of professional competence: Managing subtle cases of clinical incompetence. *Professional Psychology: Research and Practice, 21*, 462–69.

P.H.P. v. Hillingdon London Borough (1998), E.W.J. No. 2953.

Peterson, D.R. & Bry, B.H. (1980). Dimensions of perceived competence in professional psychology. *Professional Psychology: Research and Practice, 11*, 965–71.

Pettifor, J.L. (1989). Did Hamlet need a Canadian code of ethics for psychologists? *Canadian Psychology, 30*, 708–11.

Pettifor, J.L. (1996). Ethics: Virtue and politics in the science and practice of psychology. *Canadian Psychology, 37*, 1–12.

Pettifor, J.L. (1998). The Canadian Code of Ethics for Psychologists: A moral context for ethical decision making in emerging areas of practice. *Canadian Psychology, 39*, 231–38.

Pettifor, J.L. (2001). Are professional codes of ethics relevant for multicultural counselling? *Canadian Journal of Counselling, 35*, 26–35.

Pope, K.S. (1990). Therapist-patient sexual involvement: A review of the research. *Clinical Psychology Review, 10*, 477–90.

Pope, K. S., Levenson, H., & Schover, L.R. (1979). Sexual intimacy in psychology training: Results and implications of a national survey. *American Psychologist, 34*, 682–89.

Prilleltensky, I. (1990). Enhancing the social ethics of psychology: Toward a psychology at the service of social change. *Canadian Psychology, 31*, 310–19.

R. v. Beharriell (1995), 130 D.L.R. (4th) 422.

R. v. R. (K.A.) (1993), 121 N.S.R. (2d) 242.

R. v. R. S. (1985), 19 C.C.C. (3d) 115.

R. G. v. Christison (1996), S.J. No. 702.

Raquepaw, J. & Miller, R.S. (1989). Psychotherapist burnout: A componential analysis. *Professional Psychology: Research and Practice, 20,* 32–36.

Rawls, J. (1971). *A theory of justice.* Cambridge: Harvard University Press.

Reibl v. Hughes (1980), 14 C.C.L.T. 1 (S.C.C.).

Robinson, G. & Merav, A. (1976). Informed consent: Recall by patients tested postoperatively. *Annals of Thoracic Surgery, 22,* 209–12.

Robson v. Robson (1969), 2 O.R. 857.

Rozovsky, L.E. & Rozovsky, F.A., (1990). *The Candian law of consent to treatment.* Toronto: Butterworths.

Rupert, P.A. & Holmes, D.L. (1997). Dual relationships in higher education: Professional and institutional guidelines. *Journal of Higher Education, 68,* 660–78.

Schmid, D., Appelbaum, P.S., Roth, L.H., & Lidz, C. (1983). Confidentiality in psychiatry: A study of the patient's view. *Hospital and Community Psychiatry, 34,* 353–55.

Seitz, J. & O'Neill, P. (1996). Ethical decision-making and the code of ethics of the Canadian Psychological Association. *Canadian Psychology, 37,* 23–30.

Seto, M.C. (1995). Sex with therapy clients: Its prevalence, potential consequences and implications for psychologists. *Canadian Psychology, 34,* 70–86.

Sinclair, C. (1993). Codes of ethics and standards of practice. In K.S. Dobson & D.J.G. Dobson (Eds.), *Professional psychology in Canada.* Toronto: Hogrefe & Huber.

Sinclair, C. (1998). Nine unique features of the Canadian Code of Ethics for Psychologists. *Canadian Psychology, 39,* 167–76.

Sinclair, C. & Pettifor, J.L. (2001). *Companion manual to the Canadian code of ethics for psychologists,* 3rd ed. (pp. 105–43). Ottawa: Canadian Psychological Association.

Sinclair, C., Poizner, S., Gilmour-Barrett, K., & Randall, D. (1987). The development of a code of ethics for psychologists. *Canadian Psychology, 28,* 1–8.

Sinclair, C., Simon, N.P., & Pettifor, J.L. (1996). The history of ethical codes and licensure. In L.J. Bass, S.T. DeMers, J.R.P. Ogloff, C. Peterson, J.L. Pettifor, R.P. Reaves, T. Retfalvi, N.P. Simon, C. Sinclair, & R.M. Tipton (Eds.), *Professional conduct and discipline in psychology* (pp. 1–15). Washington: American Psychological Association.

Smith, D. & Fitzpatrick, M. (1995). Patient-therapist boundary issues: An integrative review of theory and research. *Professional Psychology: Research and Practice, 26,* 499–506.

Smith, E.J. & Vasquez, M.J.T. (1985). Introduction. *Counseling Psychologist, 13,* 531–36.

Smith v. Jones [1990] 1 S.C.R. 455.

Snell v. Farrell (1990), 72 D.L.R. (4th) 289.

Sonne, J., Meyer, C.B., Borys, D., & Marshall, V. (1985). Clients' reactions to sexual intimacy in therapy. *American Journal of Orthopsychiatry, 55,* 183–89.

S.T. v. Gaskell (1997), O.J. No. 2029.

Stewart v. Noone (1992), BCJ No. 1017.

Sue, D.W. (2001). Multidimensional facets of cultural competence. *The Counseling Psychologist, 29*, 790–821.

Tarasoff v. Regents of the University of California, (1976), 17 Cal.3d 425, 551 P.2d 334.

Thoreson, R., Miller, M., & Krauskopf, C. (1989). The distressed psychologist: Prevalence and treatment considerations. *Professional Psychology: Research and Practice, 20*, 153–58.

Truscott, D. & Crook, K.H. (1993). Tarasoff in the Canadian context: Wenden and the duty to protect. *Canadian Journal of Psychiatry, 38*, 84–89.

Tymchuk, A.J. (1997). Informing for consent: Concepts and methods. *Canadian Psychology, 38*, 55–75.

VandeCreek, L., Miars, R.D., & Herzog, C.E. (1987). Client anticipations and preferences for confidentiality of records. *Journal of Counseling Psychology, 34*, 62–67.

Weinberger, A. (1989). Ethics: Code value and application. *Canadian Psychology, 30*, 77–85.

Weithorn, L.A. & Campbell, S. (1982). The competency of children and adolescents to make informed treatment decisions. *Child Development, 53*, 1589–99.

Welfel, E.R. (1998). *Casebook for ethics in counseling and psychotherapy: Standards, research, and emerging issues.* Pacific Cove, CA: Brooks/Cole.

Wenden v. Trikha (1991), 8 C.C.L.T. (2d) 138 (Alta. Q.B.); aff'd. (1993) 14 C.C.L.T. (2d) 225.

Wolfe, M. (1978). Childhood and privacy. In I. Altman & J.R. Wohlwill (Eds.), *Human behavior and environment: Advances in theory and research* (Vol. 3, pp. 175–222). New York: Plenum.

Woody, R.H. (1998). Bartering for psychological services. *Professional Psychology: Research and Practice, 29*, 174–78.

Woody, R.H. (1999). Domestic violations of confidentiality. *Professional Psychology: Research and Practice, 30*, 607–10.

Wrenn, C.G. (1962). The culturally encapsulated counselor. *Harvard Educational Review, 32*, 444–49.

Wright, M.J. (1974). CPA: The first ten years. *Canadian Psychologist, 15*, 112–31.

Yalom, I. (1996). *Lying on the couch.* New York: Basic.

Yates, R.A., Yates, R.W., & Baines, P. (2000). *Introduction to law in Canada.* Scarborough: Prentice-Hall.

Youth Criminal Justice Act, 2002, c.1.

Index

About the Authors

Derek Truscott received his Ph.D. in clinical psychology from the University of Windsor in 1989. He has practiced psychology in psychiatric hospitals, rehabilitation centres, and in private practice. He is currently an Associate Professor of Counselling Psychology in the Department of Educational Psychology at the University of Alberta. He has published and presented extensively on life-threatening behaviour, psychotherapeutic processes, ethics, and standards of practice.

Kenneth Crook is a partner in the Vancouver law firm of Alexander, Holburn, Beaudin and Lang. His past practice has consisted largely of trial work for insurance clients. He has lectured and written extensively in the areas of insurance law, civil procedure, and medical malpractice.